JOURNAL OF LEGAL PLURALISM
and Unofficial Law

NUMBER 62 / 2010

Bibliographic information published by the Deutsche Nationalbibliothek
The Deutsche Nationalbibliothek lists this publication in the Deutsche Nationalbibliografie; detailed bibliographic data are available in the Internet at http://dnb.d-nb.de.

ISSN 0732-9113
ISBN 978-3-643-99895-8

A catalogue record for this book is available from the British Library

Klosbachstr. 107
CH-8032 Zürich
Tel. +41 (0) 44-251 75 05
Fax +41 (0) 44-251 75 06
e-Mail: zuerich@lit-verlag.ch
http://www.lit-verlag.ch

LIT VERLAG Dr. W. Hopf
Berlin 2011
Fresnostr. 2
D-48159 Münster
Tel. +49 (0) 2 51-620 320
Fax +49 (0) 2 51-922 60 99
e-Mail: lit@lit-verlag.de
http://www.lit-verlag.de

Distribution:
In Germany: LIT Verlag Fresnostr. 2, D-48159 Münster
Tel. +49 (0) 2 51-620 32 22, Fax +49 (0) 2 51-922 60 99, e-mail: vertrieb@lit-verlag.de

In Austria: Medienlogistik Pichler-ÖBZ, e-mail: mlo@medien-logistik.at

In the UK: Global Book Marketing, e-mail: mo@centralbooks.com

JOURNAL OF LEGAL PLURALISM
and Unofficial Law

POLICY

The Journal of Legal Pluralism and Unofficial Law (JLP) is a refereed, independent, inter-disciplinary, international journal devoted to scholarly writing, documentation, information on current developments, and communications about all aspects of legal pluralism and unofficial law anywhere in the world and at any time. Issues 1-18 bear the name *African Law Studies*.

MANUSCRIPTS

Manuscripts for the Journal of Legal Pluralism should be submitted to the editor-in-chief:

Melanie G. Wiber
Department of Anthropology, University of New Brunswick
P.O. Box 4400, Fredericton, N.B.
Canada E3B 5A3
Fax: (+ 01) (506) 453-5071
Email: wiber@unb.ca

or to one of the associate editors. Unless the editors are otherwise informed, submission of a manuscript implies the undertaking that it is not currently being considered by another journal and that if accepted it will be available for publication.

Manuscripts must conform to the style and other instructions contained in the JLP 'style sheet' (to be found on the JLP web site under the title 'Author guidelines'), and should generally be submitted in electronic form.

SUBSCRIPTIONS

From nr. 49 (2004) the Journal of Legal Pluralism has been published by LIT Verlag, Münster-Hamburg-Berlin-Vienna-London, whose address for inquiries about subscriptions and for orders is Grevener St./Fresnostr.2, D-48159 Münster, Germany, Fax (+49) (0)251 23 19 72, vertrieb@lit-verlag.de.
Back numbers of African Law Studies and the Journal of Legal Pluralism to nr. 48 are available from William S. Hein & Co., Inc., 1285 Main Street, Buffalo, New York 14209-1987, USA.

INDEXES AND DATABASES

Articles appearing in the Journal of Legal Pluralism are indexed in the principal legal and social science indexes and online data-bases. It is planned to make available the full text of all articles published more than two years previously on the website of the Journal of Legal Pluralism at www.jlp.bham.ac.uk. Currently the site contains the full text of all articles in nrs. 15 to 57, and abstracts of articles in nrs. 43 to the current number.

CITATION

The Journal of Legal Pluralism and Unofficial Law should be cited as: *Journal of Legal Pluralism*.

CONTENTS

FROM THE EDITORS

New Editorship of the JLP

The *Journal of Legal Pluralism* is in the process of changing editors. Gordon R. Woodman, who has been the sole editor-in-chief since the publication of nr. 34 (1994) is standing down, to be replaced by Melanie G. Wiber. After the appearance of this number 62, edited by them jointly, Melanie Wiber will be become sole editor-in-chief, with Gordon Woodman becoming an Associate Editor. A largely new group of Associate Editors has already been appointed (see p. iv above), with the agreement of the previous group. It is hoped that there will be a clear continuity in the production of the Journal. Melanie Wiber has already been a guest co-editor of a number (nr. 55), and she and all the Associate Editors (including two who are continuing) have been associated with the JLP as contributors and reviewers for some time. There will be no immediate change in the appearance of the JLP, nor in its wide field of interest, which will continue to be "all aspects of legal pluralism and unofficial law anywhere in the world and at any time".

Gordon Woodman would like to record his indebtedness to the outgoing group of Associate Editors, especially the two previous editors-in chief, Richard Abel and John Griffiths, who have been immensely helpful whenever he has asked them for advice and assistance. We had hoped that they and some of the other Associate Editors might continue, but most of them are determined to retire at this time.

About this Number

This number of the JLP contains, as usual, papers from a wide range both geographically and in terms of the types of legal pluralism considered. Birgit Bräuchler focuses on the Moluccas in Indonesia, and examines issues which have arisen from the nationwide trend to revive local traditions, political units and institutions, and traditional leaders accompanying the decentralisation process after the fall of President Suharto. She emphasises throughout the issues for the observance of Human Rights posed by the observance of customary laws. The other paper concerned with an Indonesian arena, that by Rikardo Simarmata on the Mahakam Delta of East Kalimantan, considers the emergence of unofficial laws, often applied by state officials at local or regional levels, on natural resource use.

Kaius Tuori studies official and semi-official attempts to formulate restatements of those customary laws in Africa which are or may be 'officially' recognized. He takes as his principal illustration the work of A. Arthur Schiller, of the Columbia University Law School concerned with law in Ethiopia. This has a special interest for us because the Journal of Legal Pluralism began its existence in 1969 as *African Law Studies*, published by the African Law Center at Columbia University when Arthur Schiller was its director. His interest in customary law and its relationship to state law ensured a focus on legal pluralism and unofficial law from the start, and so prepared the way for the journal to expand its field of interest worldwide. It moved to the African Studies Center at UCLA in 1975, and adopted its current name shortly after Schiller's death in 1977. Tuori records the widespread failure of restatements of customary law to gain authority and to be officially employed in Africa, although it might be argued that Schiller's main aim, the development of observance and respect for customary laws, has been realized to a greater extent.

Ida Harboe Knudsen brings us to Eastern Europe, and examines the development of an unofficial market in Lithuania as a result of that state's accession to the European Union (EU). The imposition of health and hygiene regulations of EU law on market participants who lacked the resources to comply has led to markets which operate 'illegally' (in the eyes of state law), and a failure to 'make' either sellers of agricultural produce or their customers into model EU 'persons'.

Heather Douglas and Abdi Hersi take us mainly into the Moslem communities in or originating from the Yemen and East Africa. They consider the relations between, on the one hand, Islamic legal injunctions and their various interpretations, and, on the other, customary practices and beliefs of members of these communities as to the chewing of the leaves of the Khat plant. The aim is to clarify the issues confronting the laws of states, such as Australia, in which some of these communities are found today.

A Correction to JLP nr. 61

Nr. 61 included an article 'Dynamic Legal Pluralism in Indonesia: Contested Legal Orders in Contemporary Aceh', by Arskal Salim. Because of an editorial error the author's first name appears in some places as Arksal. Gordon Woodman apologises for this error, for which he alone is responsible.

The Commission on Legal Pluralism

The next international conference of the Commission on Legal Pluralism, the Jubilee Congress marking the 30th year of Commission conferences, will be held in Cape Town, South Africa, from 8 to 10 September 2011. With the central theme *Living Realities of Legal Pluralism*, it will be organised in cooperation with the Centre for Legal and Applied Research (CLEAR), the Research Chair in Customary Law, and the Chair for Comparative Law in Africa, all at the University of Cape Town (UCT). Full details may be found on the website of the Commission at www.commission-on-legal-pluralism.com, and also on the website of the UCT conference management centre at http://www.pluralismconference2011.co.za/.

Melanie Wiber
Gordon Woodman

ABSTRACTS OF ARTICLES

JLP 62: 1-42

THE REVIVAL DILEMMA: REFLECTIONS ON HUMAN RIGHTS, SELF-DETERMINATION AND LEGAL PLURALISM IN EASTERN INDONESIA

Birgit Bräuchler

On the fall of Suharto, the long-surviving authoritarian president of Indonesia, in 1998, the 'reform era' began. Quite revolutionary laws on decentralisation sought to meet international notions of democracy and human rights, and local claims to greater self-determination. The decentralisation process in Indonesia was thus accompanied by a nationwide trend to revive local traditions, political units and institutions, and traditional leaders. This paper focuses on the Moluccan islands in Eastern Indonesia, where, in addition to a revival of adat (tradition and customary law), there was a strategic move by local people to foster reconciliation after conflicts in the early post-Suharto period, mainly between Christians and Muslims.

At the international level Indonesia took account of the recently developed notions of collective human rights, including indigenous peoples' right to self-determination and autonomy, and their rights to preserve and practice their own culture. This entailed the revival and re-recognition of traditional villages (*negeri*) and the reinstallation of traditional village heads (*raja*). New decentralisation laws enabled village people as cultural collectivities to return to their village adat, but tended towards the exclusion, or non-equal treatment, of cultural outsiders

At the national level decentralisation provisions, constitutional amendments, and a Human Rights Law were enacted. These were to be implemented at the local level. However, progress was impeded by the outbreak of bloody and lengthy Christian-Muslim conflict. After a peace meeting in 2002 put an official end to the conflict, local actors hoped to build sustainable peace through the revival or strengthening of traditions, traditional leaders, structures and customary law. The *raja* as traditional leaders and potential mediators, but also part of the national government system, were to play a central role. The new national autonomy law gave such local tendencies legal support, and stated that diversity was to be acknowledged. The laws raised many issues. There were various difficulties in determining who should be *raja* in many districts, and in settling their powers. There were further questions as to whether the observance of cultural rights could be premised on fixed and static notions of culture, as to which persons should make the decisive choices, and whether adat could be reduced to writing without losing its necessary flexibility. The paper uses a study of the Honitetu district to explore these issues.

It is suggested in conclusion that an unconditional revival of adat would be counterproductive. It is argued that it is crucial to preserve the flexibility of adat in order to adapt it to changing political, social and economic circumstances and to accommodate all people living in the territories, both cultural insiders and outsiders.

JLP 62: 43-70

LEGAL PLURALISM AND MODERNIZATION: AMERICAN LAW PROFESSORS IN ETHIOPIA AND THE DOWNFALL OF THE RESTATEMENTS OF AFRICAN CUSTOMARY LAW

Kaius Tuori

This article explores the ‘law and development’ movement’s controversial impact in Ethiopia through the involvement of American law professors such as A. Arthur Schiller in the struggle between modernization and traditionalism in the 1960s and 1970s. Elsewhere in Africa there were efforts to improve the administration of law by producing restatements of customary indigenous law, but Ethiopia had opted for wholesale modernization of its legal system. Because it was claimed that the Ethiopian law reform had led to the nullification of law, Schiller attempted to produce a restatement of customary indigenous land law in order to show the viability of traditional law.

These two contradictory trends, modernization and traditionalism, are presented against the background of the intellectual currents of normative pluralism and colonialism. Schiller's work was based on the premise that legal pluralism would be the future of African law. The Ethiopian codification recognized customary law only in the norms of land tenure, which Schiller used as a pretext for his project to demonstrate that law reform based on the utilization of traditional law was possible and would successfully correct the nullification of law in rural areas.

In the end, all legal reforms were made redundant by the 1974-1975 socialist revolution in Ethiopia. The legacy of Schiller is in the development of legal pluralism. He attempted to chart a course between the subjection of indigenous law to the state legal system and its irrelevance by advocating autonomy and development within the traditional legal culture.

JLP 62: 71-93

THE INSIDERS AND THE OUTSIDERS: STANDARDIZATION AND 'FAILED' PERSON-MAKING IN A LITHUANIAN MARKET PLACE

Ido Harboe Knudsen

Since Lithuania gained membership of the European Union in 2004, the country has been subjected to EU product control and food processing standards. This article discusses the effects and outcome of the intensified food control through the example of a market place, which is characterized by a spatial division between legal and illegal sale of dairy products. The women who submit to EU standards and requirements ('the Insiders') are placed inside the market hall, whereas women engaged in the sale of uncontrolled products ('the Outsiders') stand outside the bounds of the market. The limitations of the law in practice are related to what has been referred to as a person-making through standard-making (Dunn 2005). According to Dunn the imposition of standards is meant to make a self-controlled subject who internalizes the values and standards set forth by the EU. In this article it is suggested that it is the EU´s incapability to create such persons which lead to the lack of obedience to law by the Outsiders, and occasionally by the Insiders. Legal sale is only practiced at certain times, in certain spaces and only by people who have the resources in terms of money and knowledge to adhere to EU law. A change of situation at home can lead previous legal salespeople outside the bounds of the market. It is further suggested that as long as the customers equally are not 'made' into EU-consumers, they will continue to pursue illegal and 'traditional' products outside the market, which further promotes the opportunities for illegal sale.

JLP 62: 95-114

KHAT AND ISLAMIC LEGAL PERSPECTIVES: ISSUES FOR CONSIDERATION

Heather Douglas and Abdi Hersi

The leaves of the Khat plant are chewed for their stimulatory effect by many people who live around the Red Sea. People from this area have migrated throughout the world, bringing the practice with them. Consequently many countries have needed to address the question whether khat should be regulated. We argue here that, because khat use is mainly associated with Muslim people, the Islamic law about khat is also an important consideration in this debate. Accordingly this article explores the position of khat under Islamic law. In addition to a study of sources of Islamic shari'a, we have conducted focus groups with Somali people who had settled in Australia, and participants' views are considered.

Across the Muslim world opinion is sharply divided amongst Islamic scholars and Muftis on the correct approach to khat. The three main positions on khat are that it is halal (permissible), makruh (detested or discouraged) or haram (forbidden). It may be shown that each view has some support in the scholarly literature of Islam. Each was accepted by some members of the focus groups. Most of those who participated in the focus groups had a strong view on the correct position pursuant to Islam and this view influenced their decision to support or reject prohibition and to chew or not to chew khat.

This supports the claim that legal pluralism is a reality in Australia. In countries like Australia that purport to allow the free exercise of religion, prohibition of khat use may have implications for this freedom for some individuals. If khat is seen by some Muslims as an accepted part of cultural life and Muslim religious activity, targeting khat may then be seen as targeting these communities. Given that the overwhelming majority of khat users in Australia and other common law states are Muslim immigrants, the uncertain status of khat in Islam poses significant challenges to policy makers in immigrant receiving nations. As these communities' cultural norms are, to a large extent, derived from the Islamic religion, any government response to the use of khat should take into consideration these religious and cultural norms.

JLP 62: 115-146

LEGAL COMPLEXITY IN NATURAL RESOURCE MANAGEMENT IN THE FRONTIER MAHAKAM DELTA OF EAST KALIMANTAN, INDONESIA

Rikardo Simarmata

It is widely perceived that many governments in developing countries do not exercise effectively their resource control strategies over natural resources use. In coastal areas in particular control has been ineffective on a large scale. As a result in these jurisdictions coastal resource use continues to occur with little or no compliance with existing laws and regulations. Two primary conditions that facilitate such noncompliance include a lack of legal implementation and law enforcement, and administrative competition. Local government officials, particularly street-level bureaucrats, have tended not to hold resource users responsible for noncompliance with formal rules, but instead have tended to sympathize with resource users and report that they understand the reasons for non compliance. This attitude often leads to the establishment of actual resource tenure. This article describes the many arguments that local government officials in Kutai Kartanegara district, Kalimantan, Indonesia, have presented to justify their support of actual resource use. The article analyses why government officials at the local level may sympathize so strongly with actual resource use, and analyses the likely implications of these views on the coastal mangrove ecosystem in the area.

ABOUT THE CONTRIBUTORS

Birgit BRÄUCHLER is an assistant professor at the Institute for Ethnology, Goethe-University, Frankfurt-am-Main, Germany, and also works with the Asia Research Institute at the National University of Singapore. She is editor of: *Reconciling Indonesia*: *Grassroots Agency for Peace*. Abingdon UK and New York: Routledge, 2009; co-editor with John Postill of *Theorising Media and Practice*. Oxford and New York: Berghahn Books, 2010; and co-editor with Thomas Widlok of *Die Revitalisierung von Tradition / The Revitalisation of Tradition,* Zeitschrift für Ethnologie Special Issue 132, 2007. She is the author of articles and book chapters on the globalisation of local conflicts, the revival of tradition, cyberanthropology, and religion and the internet. The focus of her current research is the cultural dimension of reconciliation in Indonesia.

Heather DOUGLAS is an Associate Professor in the TC Beirne School of Law, The University of Queensland, Australia. From 2001-2007 she was a part-time commissioner with the Queensland Law Reform Commission, and in 2004 she was a visiting scholar at the Centre for Socio-Legal Studies, Oxford University. She teaches and researches in the criminal justice field. For the past two years she has been looking at the regulation of the drug khat in Australia. She is particularly interested in the relationship between indigenous people and the criminal law. Work she has published related to these fields include: (with Merali Pedder) 'Legal Regulation of the Drug Khat in Australia' 18 *Journal of Law and Medicine* 18: 284-301 (2010); (with Jennifer Corrin) 'A Tragedy of Monumental Proportions': Indigenous Australians and the Sentencing Process' (2010) *Social and Legal Studies* 19(2): 197-216 (2010); and (with John Chesterman) 'Law on Australia's Northern Frontier: The Fall and Rise of Race' 24 (1) *Canadian Journal of Law and Society* 24(1): 69-83 (2009). She was awarded the degree of PhD in 2006 for a thesis exploring the work of Justice Martin Kriewaldt, the sole judge of the Northern Territory Supreme Court of Australia during the 1950s.

Ida HARBOE KNUDSEN, who was born in Ålborg, Denmark, 1977, is a Research Fellow at the Max Planck Institute for Social Anthropology in Halle/ Saale, Germany, and an associate researcher at the Vytautas Magnas University, Kaunas, Lithuania. She studied Ethnography and Social Anthropology at Århus University, Denmark, from 1999 to 2006. From 2006–2010 she was a doctoral student in the Project Group Legal Pluralism at the Max Planck Institute, Halle/Saale, financed by the EU sponsored programme, Marie Curie SocAnth, and was awarded the PhD for a dissertation on the effects of legal changes in the Lithuanian countryside after the country's entry into the EU. Her research interests continue to be around the themes of legal change, post-socialism, the EU and its new member states, and social security. She has published: 'Trade and Exchange among Farmers in a Post-Soviet Lithuanian Village.' Pp. 10-29 in *Defining Region: Socio-Cultural Anthropology and Interdisciplinary Perspectives*, Klaipeda University (2006); 'Who represents who? - a critical approach to Lithuanian identity discourse.' Pp. 59-68 in *Identity Politics, Histories, Regions and Borderlands, in Acta Historica XIX, Studia Antropologica III,* Klaipeda University (2009); and is about to publish: 'Keletas pasvarstymų apie žmogaus amžių, politiką ir politikus kaimo bendruomenėje, Lietuvai įstojus į ES [Some Reflections About Age, Politics and Rural Politicians after Lithuania´s entry into the EU].' In *Lietuvos Etnologija* (forthcoming).

Abdi HERSI holds a Master's degree in International Studies from the University of Queensland, Australia, and is currently a PhD candidate at Griffith University, Australia, working on the topic 'Understanding the meanings of integration: Perspectives of Muslims, members of the wider public and the state'. His research interests include immigrant incorporation in general and in particular the integration of Muslim immigrants and refugees from Sub-Saharan Africa. He has worked for the Australian Commonwealth Department of Immigration and Citizenship, where he has observed settlement services and processes that refugees and immigrants go through in their adjustment to host societies. Before migrating to Australia, he worked for the International Organisation for Migration and the Australian High Commission in Kenya, assisting in pre-departure cultural orientation programmes for immigrants and refugees bound for Australia, the United States and Canada. In Australia, he has worked on research projects that studied the new and emerging African communities in Australia. He is currently a member of the Advisory Board of Queensland African Communities Council, Inc.

Rikardo SIMARMATA is working as a Ph.D researcher at Van Vollenhoven Institute for Law, Governance and Development, Leiden University, the Netherlands. He holds a first degree in law. He spent eights years as an NGO activist working for issues on land and indigenous peoples rights. His doctoral work is focused on law making and legal implementation of resource tenure rights. He has published numerous articles and books over the past ten years concerning forest tenure and indigenous peoples. His recent publication is *The Struggle for Truth and Justice A Survey of Transitional Justice Initiatives Throughout Indonesia*, New York: International Center for Transitional Justice (2004), and (in Bahasa Indonesia) *Legal Recognition of Indigenous Peoples in Indonesia*, Jakarta:

Regional Initiative on Indigenous Peoples' Rights and Development-UNDP (2006). He can be contacted at simarmatar@cbn.net.id or r.simarmata@law.leidenuniv.nl.

Kaius TUORI (born 1974) is Senior Researcher at the Center of Excellence in Global Governance Research, Faculty of Law, University of Helsinki, Finland. He holds a doctorate in legal history and a MA in history, both from Helsinki, and has research interests in legal history, legal anthropology and archaeology. His publications include *Ancient Roman Lawyers and Modern Legal Ideals* (2007) and numerous articles.

THE REVIVAL DILEMMA: REFLECTIONS ON HUMAN RIGHTS, SELF-DETERMINATION AND LEGAL PLURALISM IN EASTERN INDONESIA[1]

Birgit Bräuchler

> Anthropologists analyse competing legal registers, each with its own historical trajectory and historical consequences. They view legal pluralism in the light of historical struggles over sovereignty, nationhood and legitimacy (Vincent 2002: 332).

Introduction

For many reasons, Indonesia provides excellent case studies to discuss the complexity and contradictions of current debates on human rights and cultural self-determination: the country's fragmented and multi-ethnic composition, its political transformation during the last decade, its role in the 'Asian values' debate and its

[1] I would like to thank the Asia Research Institute, National University of Singapore, for supporting this research project and the Royal Netherlands Institute of Southeast Asian and Caribbean Studies (KITLV) and the Van Vollenhoven Institute in Leiden for providing me the opportunity to discuss and revise a draft version of this paper. I also thank Franz von Benda-Beckmann and Gordon Woodman for their inspiring feedback and valuable comments and suggestions on an earlier version.

vivid human rights activist culture.[2] Pressured by internal rebellion and an international human rights lobby, the long-lasting authoritarian president of Indonesia, Suharto, had to step back in 1998, an act which rang in the so-called *era reformasi*. Quite revolutionary laws on decentralisation tried to meet international notions of democracy and human rights and, at the same time, local claims for more self-determination with regard to political representation, culture and resource use. The decentralisation process in Indonesia was thus accompanied by a nationwide trend to revive local traditions, political units and institutions, and traditional leaders. This paper is mainly concerned with the Moluccan islands in Eastern Indonesia, that are especially interesting, since the revival of adat (tradition and customary law) in this area was not only part of the common trend in Indonesia. It was also a strategic move by local people to foster reconciliation after one of the most violent and long-lasting post-Suharto conflicts fought out there from 1999 until 2003, as a result of a strategic mobilisation process, mainly between Christians and Muslims. The Moluccas provide an illuminating case to discuss the challenging and problematic nature of the revival of tradition and the implementation of cultural self-determination in the current democratisation process in Indonesia.

I will outline three levels concerned in the pluralistic legal constitution of the Moluccas and the processes that are of interest for my argument: the international, the national and the local. The closer I get to the local, my field site in the Central Moluccas, the more detailed these analyses get. Only very briefly will I sketch the international rise of collective and cultural human rights and some of the problems involved such as exclusivism. This will serve as a general discussion to the main issues that will be taken up in the national and local sections. Next follow reflections on a national level about the current transition to a more decentralised state, the accompanying re-emergence of 'old elites' (accompanied, in turn, by exclusivism), the human rights situation and the problematic nature of a definition of 'indigenous people' in Indonesia. Most time is then spent on a critical analysis of the implementation of the new laws in the Central Moluccas at the local level (province, district, village). I will first provide some historical background, introduce the conflict situation and the decentralisation process in the Moluccas

[2] The 'Asian values' debate, among others, revolves around the rejection of a Western human rights imperialism. For details and critique see: Bruun and Jacobsen 2000: 2; Chan 2000: 60; Christie and Roy 2001: Introduction; Cowan et al. 2001b: 6-7; Eysink 2006; Forsythe and McMahon 2003: 306; Horowitz and Schnabel 2004: 9; Jacobsen and Bruun 2000.

and then elaborate on the translation of the new national laws into regional and local contexts and regulations. In focus are the revival and re-recognition of traditional villages (*negeri*) and the reinstallation of traditional village heads (*raja*). The new decentralisation laws enabled village people as cultural collectivities to return to their village adat, an example of the return of (collective) cultural rights to a group of people (in this case 'indigenous people' or rather *masyarakat adat* in the Central Moluccas).[3] Part of the village culture is the return of (in some cases) formerly feudal hereditary leaders and the exclusion, or rather non-equal treatment of cultural outsiders. Both of these contradict the individual's human right on egalitarianism, at least from an international human rights perspective. As the notion of legal pluralism implies, international human rights law, state law, religious law and customary law often coexist, although they might not share each other's (legal) values (F von Benda-Beckmann 2009: 123). Legal pluralism does not necessarily imply peaceful coexistence of the various legal systems that are rooted in different settings (the international, the national, the local), but all come to the fore in the local context where their relationship is constantly negotiated as the case studies presented in this paper illustrate. I will here discuss the challenges of the right to self-determination and culture (embodied in the revival of tradition), addressing questions of representation and agency, codification and essentialisation, authenticity and exclusion. A brief village case study exemplifies not only how some Moluccans try to cope with these challenges, but also how certain groups of people (migrants) who are not (allowed to be) part of these developments are excluded. Drawing on ethnographic fieldwork I conducted during several stays in the Central Moluccas (a district of the Moluccan province) between 2002 and 2008, I aim to move away from a prevailing overly legalistic and political science understanding of human rights, and illustrate and stress the value of an anthropological look at these problems. This article also aims to problematise the static notion of culture involved in these debates. The dilemma of

[3] For an explanation see below. Although adat is a holistic concept that both denotes the traditional way of life of a cultural group and the law practiced within this group, the second dimension is not explicitly dealt with yet in the new law on decentralisation and its implementation in the regions. There is thus still a lot of uncertainty about how to deal with issues of (criminal) law on the local level. As argued by Lee, law had already been analytically separated from adat by the colonial powers and the attempts of Dutch scholars to write down, but also instrumentalise adat as law "as a means to undercut Islamic law, and also as a useful way to encompass and at the same time keep clear of the administration of local justice" (Lee 1999: 70, also 75).

flexible cultural traits and traditions and the need to fix them in order to codify and (seemingly) protect them is a central theme. The paper concludes with some reflections on cultural flexibility, human rights and legal pluralism that are of importance for the analysis of the processes here described.

The International: Human Rights, Collective Rights, Cultural Rights

With the increasing emphasis in the 1980s and 1990s on the cultural dimension of the human rights debate, collective rights came into the foreground, in particular indigenous rights – the so-called fourth generation of human rights (Messer 1993: 222-223). The International Labor Organization set a first marker in 1989 by formulating Convention No. 169 on Indigenous and Tribal Peoples in Independent Countries (ILO 169). One of the more recent trailblazing achievements in this decade-long debate was the adoption of a Draft Declaration on the Rights of Indigenous Peoples (1994, revised in 2006) by the United Nations General Assembly on September 13, 2007 (UNDRIP), with a majority of 143 votes in favour, four against and eleven abstentions.[4] Apart from indigenous peoples' right to self-determination and autonomy or self-government in matters relating to their internal and local affairs (Article 3 and 4), the UNDRIP emphasizes their right "to practice and revitalise their cultural traditions and customs" (Article 11.1), "to maintain, control, protect and develop their cultural heritage, traditional knowledge and traditional cultural expressions" (Article 31.1), and "to determine the structures and to select the membership of their institutions in accordance with their own procedures" (Article 33.2), including juridical systems and customs, as long as they are in accordance with international human rights standards (Article 34) – to mention only a few of the articles that are of interest for this particular paper and its focus on self-determination and the revival of tradition in Indonesia and the Moluccas.

The enormous challenge is "to achieve unity in basic human rights practices without destroying cultural diversity" (Messer 1993: 232). We are caught in an alleged paradox, that we somehow have to translate the human rights system with its original emphasis on individualism, bodily integrity and equality into the

---

[4] http://www.iwgia.org/sw248.asp, 14.11.2007. For a very helpful overview of indigenous communities in Indonesian (national) legislation see Bedner and Huis 2008. For a more general recent discussion of the concept of indigeneity see: Barnard 2006; Guenther et al. 2006; Kuper 2003.

frameworks and standards of local cultures and contexts that are often shaped in terms of collective rights, to which individuals have to subordinate themselves (see also Merry 2005: 38-39); collective rights that are now reformulated as human rights. The enforcement of collective rights is necessary for the survival of cultures, but can also bear dangers, especially when they are seen as compatible or even superior to individual rights: Collective rights can become exclusivist rights, marginalizing categories of individuals who are external to a specific local community where they live, but are nonetheless part of the same nation state (Howard 1992: 97-98; compare also Kuper 2003: 390). I will exemplify this later with the migrant population in the area under study.

A major dilemma in the thinking about human rights, according to Franz von Benda-Beckmann, is the problem of their representation. The consequence of opposing human rights identified with 'the West' and culture identified with 'the rest' is "that little attention has been given to the fact that both human rights and culture (however it may be defined) in most parts of the world coexist with a variety of legal forms (legal pluralism)" and that people are forced "into the strategic essentialising that the categories of international law demand from them for 'recognition'" (F von Benda-Beckmann 2009: 122, 125). This has become even more precarious since the international promotion of a human right to culture. As Sieder and Witchell in Cowan et al.'s edited volume on anthropological perspectives on culture and rights show, and what becomes most obvious in the Moluccan case study, both cultural activists or social movements and policy makers tend to essentialise indigenous culture (Sieder and Witchell 2001; Cowan et al. 2001a: 150). The problem is that local communities or indigenous groups often have to prove that they still live their 'traditional lifestyle' by somehow substantiating 'cultural authenticity', which often implies a static and essentialised notion of culture, in order to be accorded collective/indigenous rights.[5] However, a prerequisite for constructing the possibilities of action (Merry 2006: 9) and the successful mediation between a universalistic human rights concept and local culture is the dismissal of culture as something reified and essentialised and the emphasis on an open and flexible notion of culture, as has been promoted by social anthropologists for the last decades.

[5] See, for instance: Cowan 2001: 171, 2006: 17; Gellner 2001: 177; Guenther et al. 2006: 24; Merry 2001: 39, 42; Sieder and Witchell 2001: 201-207.

The National: 'Unity in Diversity', Decentralisation and Human Rights in Indonesia

> In its ambiguous and protean character, by turns progressive and reactionary, emancipating and authoritarian, idealistic and manipulative, adat revivalism in some ways epitomizes the paradoxes of the post-New Order era. ... an era in which unprecedented political freedom and strikingly successful formal democratization ... have gone hand in hand with ethnic violence outside the electoral sphere, burgeoning corruption, continued radical failure of legal and judicial institutions, and strong persistence of New Order military, bureaucratic and business interests in most areas of political life (Henley and Davidson 2007: 18).

In general, the democratisation process in Indonesia had a rather miserable start. With the stepping down of its authoritarian president Suharto (1966-1998), several long suppressed economic, political, social, ethnic and religious conflicts all over Indonesia erupted. Whilst cases with a separatist background such as Aceh, Papua and East Timor dominate international headlines, large-scale violence that occurred in Kalimantan, Poso (Sulawesi) and the Moluccas are usually only mentioned in passing on an international level.[6] Human rights violations were always part of practical policy in Indonesia, be it the introduction of 'guided democracy' by its first president Sukarno in 1959, the mass killings of 1965 where hundreds of thousands of alleged communists were massacred, the invasion of East Timor in 1975 after the Portuguese had left the country, the Dili massacre in 1991, the restriction on political parties and the freedom of the press, the killing of alleged sorcerers in East Java in the 1990s, or the constant human rights violations in Papua and Aceh – to mention just a few. More implicit violations of human rights were unification efforts. The motto of the Indonesian state *Bhinneka Tunggal Ika* (unity in diversity) only very superficially accommodated the cultural plurality of the country. Important instruments to foster both unification and the

[6] For analyses of the conflicts in Kalimantan and Poso see, for example: Acciaioli 2001; Aragon 2001; Davidson 2008. Another case that made it into international headlines is the murder of the prominent human rights activist Munir in 2004. For current human rights violations in Indonesia see e.g. U.S. Department of State 2006. For human rights in Indonesia see also Juwana 2006; and Hadiprayitno 2010.

Suharto regime's power were the military as the preserver of national unity, transmigration programmes mainly transferring people from overpopulated Java to the outer Islands, and "a national edifice of territorial control" (Thorburn 2003) that was initiated with Law No. 5 of 1974 on Regional Government (*Undang-undang no. 5 tahun 1974 tentang pokok-pokok pemerintahan di daerah*, UU 5/1974) and culminated in the village law No. 5 of 1979 (*Undang-undang no. 5 tahun 1979 tentang pemerintahan desa*, UU 5/1979), which resulted in the standardisation or javanisation of governmental structures all over Indonesia from the top down to the village level. Reactions in the Moluccas towards the law differed from acceptance to resistance and a very superficial implementation (see e.g. Bartels 1977; Cooley 1961; Pannell 2003: 28; Pariela 1996). After the colonial period had already had severe impacts on the sociocultural organisation of Moluccan society (see below), UU 5/1979 further destroyed local structures and autonomous village units, marginalised traditional functionaries and institutions as well as customary law, and deprived them of their meaning (Fauzi and Zakaria 2002; Kato 1989; Thorburn 2003). Only after the stepping down of Suharto in 1998 did the doors open for the (re)constitution of local communities' autonomy, the introduction of democratic values into the Indonesian state structure, and the opening up towards human rights. This became evident in three instances: the passing of laws on decentralisation in 1999 and 2004, constitutional amendments in 2000, and the passing of the Human Rights Law in 1999.

Decentralisation Law

In the long run, the Indonesian government could not withstand internal and external pressures, which were to a large extent influenced by the international human rights and democratisation discourse. The 1990s in Indonesia saw a decisive opening up of space for social movements which finally resulted in substantive upheavels and the 'resignation' of the authoritarian Suharto regime in May 1998. In 1999 laws on the devolution of political authority (No. 22) and fiscal decentralisation (No. 25) were passed under the interim president B.J. Habibie replacing UU 5/1974 and UU 5/1979, which was declared as not being in accordance with Indonesia's 1945 Constitution (Fauzi and Zakaria 2002: 8-9). The main beneficiaries of the new decentralisation law in Indonesia's territorial government structure were the districts (*kabupaten*) and the villages (*desa*), not the larger provinces (*provinsi*), in order to prevent any separatist tendencies (F and K von Benda-Beckmann 2001: 2; Kreuzer 2002: 25; Schulte Nordholt 2003: 564-565). The authorities started to implement the 1999 laws in 2001 and revised them with law No. 32 and 33 respectively in 2004 (UU 32 & 33/2004). The new legislation has been one important step on the way to a more democratic Indonesia and towards granting the right to self-determination to the Indonesian people. Chapter XI of UU 32/2004 is dedicated to the village level, the focus of my attention.[7]

As mentioned before, one significant effect of the new decentralisation policies was the emergence of adat revival movements throughout Indonesia. At first glance, it looks as if national and international human rights activists and local people fighting for more autonomy and self-determination and indigenous peoples' rights have finally gained considerable ground. But a closer look reveals that these developments are highly ambiguous and not only an indication of a new and open pluralism in Indonesia, but also of exclusivism and divisiveness.[8] On the one hand, the new law enables the re-strengthening or rediscovery of local traditions, identities, political structures (such as the *nagari* in West Sumatra and the *negeri* in the Moluccas) and traditional local mechanisms of integration and conflict resolution that might both foster peace and democracy. Moreover, it allows for important steps towards a more just access to resources, thus putting an end to the central government's exclusive exploitation of local resources. But, on the other hand, the revival of adat also fosters conflict and exclusion and, in some places, legitimises the re-emergence of authoritarian local elites. The main issue here are campaigns for and self-promotion of local people, the so-called *putra daerah*, "to control local government and secure preferential treatment for their communities in the allocation of economic resources and government positions" (Aspinall and Fealy 2003: 6) - be it the sultans in the Northern Moluccas, Dayak elites in Kalimantan, *nagari* elites in Minangkabau, the Malay elite in Riau or *raja* in the

[7] For a more general overview of the new legislation, its diverse effects, and a history of decentralisation politics in Indonesia see, for example: Aspinall and Fealy 2003; Bach 2003; Kivimäki et al. 2002.

[8] For a good discussion of the ambiguity of adat revivalism in post-Suharto Indonesia, including case studies from various regions in Indonesia, see Davidson and Henley 2007. Besides this there is now a wealth of material available on revival movements throughout Indonesia, among them, for example: on Maluku, Bräuchler 2007, 2009a, b; on Minahasa (North Sulawesi) Jacobsen 2002a, b; on Minangkabau (West Sumatra), F and K von Benda-Beckmann 2001, 2007a, 2009; on North Maluku, Bräuchler 2007; Bubandt 2002; Klinken 2007b; and another volume comprising more case studies, Schulte Nordholt and van Klinken 2007.

Moluccas.[9] In many cases, the *putra daerah* are seen as the motors for the re-establishment of feudal structures (if such forms did exist before) and hierarchies, the exclusion of non-adat people, the instigation of local conflicts, the undermining of a national Indonesian identity, and the exploitation of natural resources.[10] The traditional leaders, whose revival and reinstallation are now legalised on certain levels, are often not democratically chosen, and genealogy is put before meritocracy, which is, at least at first sight, against any principles of individual equality, the main objective of article 2 of the Universal Declaration of Human Rights of 1948. Having said this, it must be acknowledged that these local leaders are often the most important interface between the local people and the Indonesian government. It is these leaders that can facilitate the empowerment of their people and it is they who have the potential to act as an integrative force in conflict areas through the re-employment of integrative symbols and conflict resolution and peace mechanisms.

Another (seeming) contradiction in the decentralisation process, identified by Franz and Keebet von Benda-Beckmann in West Sumatra, is that

> top-down regulation, in which the centre enacts higher legislation to be followed by implementing regulations on ever descending and smaller levels of administration goes hand-in-hand with the dynamics of relatively autonomous local politics and regulation (F and K von Benda-Beckmann 2009: 294).

Villages in West Sumatra as in the Moluccas thus have become somewhat more independent from the central and provincial administration, "yet as the lowest level of state organization, heavily regulated and predominantly funded by the districts,

[9] For Bangka-Belitung, for example, see: Permana 2002; for Kalimantan, Klinken 2007b; McCarthy 2004; for (North) Maluku, Bräuchler 2007; Bubandt 2002; Klinken 2001a, 2007b; for Riau, Bach 2003; and for West Sumatra, F and K von Benda-Beckmann 2001, 2007a, 2009. Prominent examples of how the revival of traditions and traditional leadership instigated or deepened local conflicts are the sultanates and their traditional guards in Northern Maluku (see Bubandt 2002, Klinken 2001b) and the Dayak elite in West Kalimantan (Davidson 2007).

[10] Schulte Nordholt (2003: 571) even fears "that the environment will turn out to be decentralization's hardest-hit victim." Other researchers arguing for a negative impact of the new laws on the environment include: Lounela 2004; McCarthy 2004; Resosudarmo 2003.

they remain deeply embedded in the wider Indonesian political, financial and social structures" (F and K von Benda-Beckmann 2007a: 441).

What is evident is that "with this new politics of tradition, important changes to the ways local identity is imagined and cultural politics is conducted are likely to occur in the coming years in Indonesia" (Bubandt 2002: 115). What is just as evident is that power, power struggles, competition, and intense negotiations play a prominent role in the implementation processes of the decentralisation law - on all levels. National laws have to be translated into local contexts. The first step is the composing of Government Regulations at the provincial level (Peraturan Daerah Provinsi, Perda Provinsi - e.g. Maluku) that deal with certain aspects of the new law, such, as in our case, the re-establishment of traditional political forms on the village level. This is then further adapted to a certain region through a Government Regulation at the district level (Perda Kabupaten - e.g. Central Moluccas). The last step will be to draft so-called village regulations (Perda *Negeri*, as for the Central Moluccas) that refer to local adat and can thus provide detailed information on how to implement certain aspects of national law. That's where the dilemma of codification will come in most prominently as I will lay out later. On all levels, those in charge bring along their own motivation, knowledge and interest.

Constitutional Amendments

To seemingly prove the serious nature of its efforts to foster democracy and human rights, the post-Suharto government even changed the national constitution of 1945 in 2000 (see also Hadiprayitno 2010). What was later provided in Article 2(9) of UU 32/2004 is in fact a copy of the amended Article 18B(2) of the Constitution (compare also Bedner and Huis 2008: 174):

> The Indonesian state acknowledges and respects the unity of adat law communities and their customary law as long as those are still alive and in line with the evolution of the people and the principles of the Unitary State of Indonesia, as regulated in its laws.[11]

[11] UU 32/2004, Chapter I, § 2 (9): *Negara mengakui dan menghormati kesatuan-kesatuan masyarakat hukum adat beserta hak tradisionalnya sepanjang masih hidup dan sesuai dengan perkembangan masyarakat dan prinsip Negara Kesatuan Republik Indonesia, yang diatur dalam undang-undang.*

However, this implies that, in case of doubt, the state still has the upper hand. Moreover, it is rather grotesque and contradictory to make "being alive" a condition, since it does not take the destructive forces of both colonialism and the Indonesian government into account and is also based on a rather essentialised concept of culture. The other new provision added to the 1945 Constitution, which is of direct relevance to our discussions, is chapter XA on Human Rights. In Article 28I(3) one reads that "cultural identity and the rights of traditional communities [*masyarakat tradisional*] are respected in accordance with evolution of the times and civilization".[12] This is supportive towards the granting of cultural and collective rights to indigenous people. However, as pointed out by Bedner and Huis (2008: 170), the article avoids the term "*adat* community" (*masyarakat adat*) or "*adat* law community" (*masyarakat hukum adat*), since both terms bear connotations of autonomy.

Human Rights Law

By the end of 1998, Indonesia had ratified the Convention Against Torture and other Cruel, Inhuman or Degrading Treatment or Punishment and the International Labor Organization's Convention No. 87 Concerning Freedom of Association and Protection of the Right to Organize. Restrictions concerning the formation of political parties were lifted and the mass media were granted freedom of expression (Christie and Roy 2001: 130). In 1999 the Indonesian government passed law No. 39 on Human Rights, which explicitly mentions that local adat, including traditional land rights, has to be acknowledged and protected by the law, the people and the government.[13] In 2005 and 2006 Indonesia ratified both the Covenant on Civil and Political Rights and that on Economic, Social and Cultural Rights (Eysink 2006: 9). As outlined above, the UNDRIP was also approved by Indonesia.

[12] UU Dasar Republik Indonesia, Chapter XA, § 28I (3): *Identitas budaya dan hak masyarakat tradisional dihormati selaras dengan perkembangan zaman dan peradaban.*

[13] UU 39/1999, Chapter II, § 6: *Dalam rangka penegakan hak asasi manusia, perbedaan dan kebutuhan dalam masyarakat hukum adat harus diperhatikan dan dilindungi oleh hukum, masyarakat, dan Pemerintah. Identitas budaya masyarakat hukum adat, termasuk hak atas tanah ulayat dilindungi, selaras dengan perkembangan zaman.* For a more detailed analysis of this article see Bedner and Huis 2008: 176-177.

The definition and delineation of indigenous people in Indonesia is, however, highly problematic due to its history and composition. "Indigenous people" is translated as "*masyarakat adat*" (adat community) in the Indonesian version of the UNDRIP as well as in the Indigenous Peoples Alliance of the Indonesian Archipelago (Aliansi Masyarakat Adat Nusantara, AMAN).[14] It is likely that almost nobody in Indonesia would claim not to be an adat person, which would amount to being without culture and uncivilized. More and more groups apply for AMAN membership that multiplied from a handful of members when it was founded in 1999 to more than thousand in 2007.[15] One main criterion for AMAN is that those people have a specific, culturally determined relationship to the land they inhabit that goes back to ancestral times. As argued by Bedner and Huis, "many local movements citing *adat* to legitimize their struggle for more autonomy and resources do not label themselves 'indigenous peoples'"; however, "a large number of such communities would fall within the ILO definitions and some have used the opportunities this offers" (Bedner and Huis 2008: 166). In the UNDRIP "indigenous people" is not defined at all. For this contribution I therefore consider those people in the Central Moluccas as indigenous (including the islands of Ambon, Lease and West Seram), who already inhabited the area I am talking about long before the arrival of European traders and colonial powers, and that claim to originate from a mountain called Nunusaku on the mother island Seram. As outlined above, the more general provincial implementation of the national decentralisation laws is to be translated into the terminology of the various cultural areas, in this case the Central Moluccas (see next section). Since the villages are usually considered the main source for one's (group/cultural) identity in the Moluccan province, those regional regulations are translated again into village regulations. The migrant population, most prominently the Butonese from South Sulawesi, some of whom have been living in Moluccan villages for generations, are not considered to be adat people either from the perspective of local (indigenous) communities or according to the new decentralisation law (for more details on the migrant issue see below).

---

[14] For an interpretation of such a translation, though in another context, see Henley and Davidson 2007: 28.

[15]Compare http://ccmin.aippnet.org/index.php?option=com_content&view=article&id=5&Itemid=8, 16.12.2010.

The Local: Self-Determination and the Revival of Tradition in the Moluccas

Some Historical Background

The Moluccan archipelago is inhabited by slightly more than two million people and has been divided into the Province of the Moluccas (Maluku) and the Northern Moluccas (Maluku Utara) since 1999. The islands became famous as the Spice Islands, since it was the nutmegs and cloves originating in the area that attracted the colonial powers from the 16th century onwards: the Portuguese, the Spaniards, the British, and, the most persistent ones, the Dutch.[16] It was these colonisers who brought Christianity shortly after Islam had been introduced to the area. Political power, economic profits and religion were therefore closely intertwined from the very beginning. Christians were favoured during colonial times in education and bureaucracy, which has been an issue among the Muslim part of the population until today. It was also colonial policies that led to the split of religiously mixed villages to create monoreligious villages, a decisive prerequisite for religion becoming so influential in Moluccan society and enabling people to be mobilised for the most recent mass violence. To provide an idea of how 'traditional' two of the central terms of the decentralisation era in the Moluccas are: *Raja* is a title that was part of a ranking system of village heads introduced by the Dutch, where the *raja* – an imported, formerly Malay title (Fraassen and Straver 2002: 98) – was the highest position, *patih* the second highest, and *orang kaya* the lowest. The term *negeri* was only introduced to the Moluccas through the Dutch in the 17th century, and most of these villages were reconstituted when a large part of the central Moluccan population that lived in the mountainous interior of the islands was moved to the coast in the middle of the 17th century (Leirissa et al. 1982/1983; Pariela 1996: 119; the legislation is contained in Staatsblad 19a, 1824). In this process *raja* positions were often transferred to other lineages, which were more willing to cooperate with the Dutch, and, as Keebet von Benda-Beckmann emphasizes, "territory was redistributed, leading to disputes over land between neighbouring villages that have lasted until the present" (K von Benda-Beckmann 2007: 288). Actually, much of what is currently regarded as adat structures and adat positions was largely fabricated by the colonial government (see F von Benda-

[16] This, due to restrictions of space, is only a very cursory historical introduction to the area. For more in-depth accounts see, for example: Andaya 1993; Bartels 1994; Chauvel 1990; Fraassen 1972; Knaap 1987.

Beckmann 1999, K von Benda-Beckmann 2004: 227-228); ever since then "the political organization has been an amalgam of adat principles and government regulations" (F von Benda-Beckmann 1990: 27). The result of this restructuring process was that "many of the new villages were subsequently incorporated as 'adat' by the local population, although they never fully replaced pre-colonial legal notions" (F and K von Benda-Beckmann 2008: 14-15). However, Franz and Keebet von Benda-Beckmann also warn against dangerously stereotypical "notions of colonial creations of customary adat law" as propagated by scholars such as Peter Burns (F and K von Benda-Beckmann 2008: 3; Burns 2004, 2007). This would "underrate(d) the agency of local people and overrate(d) the actual significance of the colonial legal constructions of adat or adat law on the legal life of the population" (F and K von Benda-Beckmann 2008: 4). This admonition should also be kept in mind when we look at adat constructions and/or recreations in the course of the implementation of the new decentralisation law.

The *raja* position underwent tremendous changes over the various epochs (for more details, see Bräuchler 2011). Being a primus inter pares in the village and the village adat council in pre-colonial times, s/he was instrumentalised and turned into an absolute ruler by the colonial Dutch East India Company. After the colonial government had taken over and initiated a decentralisation process in the early 20th century, the *raja* were disempowered and impoverished. Whereas after independence village adat was still kept in place, this tremendously changed during Suharto's New Order (especially after law No. 5/1979 on Village Government). All village heads were uniformely called *kepala desa* then, made head of the village parliament and had thus the final say in village politics (provided that it conformed to higher level politics). Theoretically the position was open to everybody then, although in most villages the *raja* lineages were still decisive in determining the village heads (compare also F von Benda-Beckmann 1988). Although UU 5/1979 had a strong impact on the local level, adat was not doomed to death in the Moluccas. Village people and adat functionaries found ways either to maintain their traditional institutions in parallel to the imposed governmental system (the *raja*'s function then, for example, was restricted to land issues and adat matters not interfering with the central government's structure) or to merge the two systems by, for instance, installing a former *raja* or a descendant of his lineage as the new village head, now called *kepala desa*. Such 'remnants' (which is a problematic expression in itself) of a formerly holistic adat system, where political, economic, social and legal aspects could not be isolated, constitute a necessary basis for current revitalisation efforts based on the new law on decentralisation. This law provides a chance to reinstall the 'true' *raja*, although now with restricted power as I will outline below, but this is quite problematic as this brief historical sketch already foreshadows.[17]

Conflict and Decentralisation in Maluku[18]

Despite the early politicisation of religion, there were always family ties, common ancestry and traditional mechanisms to keep the Moluccans united. One of the latter is the *pela* system in the Central Moluccas, that is alliances between two or more villages irrespective of their religion (see in particular Bartels 1977). Unlike the population in most other parts of predominantly Muslim Indonesia, a substantial part of the population of the Moluccas is constituted by Christians.[19] The region was praised for its religious harmony up until December 1998. This is why nobody really expected that a minor quarrel between a Christian bus driver and a Muslim passenger in Ambon city, the capital of the Moluccan province, in January 1999 would end in a bloody and enduring multidimensional conflict,

[17] If people in Maluku had chosen not to return to the *negeri* system introduced by the colonial powers but to pre-colonial types of settlement (*aman* or *hena*) and power structures, many of the debates and fights involved in determining the proper *raja* line could perhaps have been prevented. I assume, however, that for practical reasons it would not have been an option for Moluccans to leave their villages (*negeri*) at the coast, move back into the mountains and try to re-construct their former ways of life. The cultural community of the *negeri* is what they seem to identify with most although the former settlements still play an important role in constructing the villages' histories and cultural identities.

[18] If not mentioned otherwise, the following paragraphs are based on my field research in the Moluccas in 2002, 2005, 2006, 2007 and 2008, and interviews I conducted there on various levels with jurists, academics, NGOs, *raja*, village people, government representatives, adat functionaries and religious figures. I would like to use this opportunity to thank them all for their support, cooperation and friendship.

[19] The Muslim/Christian proportions of the population in the Central Moluccas used to be 50:50. As a result of transmigration, i.e. the migration of Muslims from other parts of Indonesia to the Moluccas, approximately 60% of the population in the province of Maluku is now Muslim, 40% Christian; in the Central Moluccan district the Muslim percentage is even higher (Badan Pusat Statistik Propinsi Maluku 2007: 108). However, this is still in contrast to a roughly 87% Muslim population in the whole of Indonesia.

which spread over the whole of the Moluccas: hundreds of churches and mosques were destroyed, thousands of people on both sides were killed, and hundreds of thousands, nearly one third of the Moluccan population, had to flee. Moluccan society became divided along religious lines in every respect, both socially and geographically. According to some observers ethnic and religious issues were instrumentalised by the Indonesian military and members of the former Suharto regime in order to mobilise the Moluccan people and agitate Muslims against Christians. Others rather stress local roots of the conflict or investigate the role of fundamentalist Islamic groups from outside the Moluccas, or the media as conflict factors.[20] What added to all this, is that local traditions fostering interreligious harmony had come under increasing pressure through the central government's policies over the last decades, namely, through its unification strategies, and its transmigration and its Islamisation programs (see, for example, Bartels 2003). What is obvious is that the Moluccan conflict was multidimensional and it took many local as well as national peace initiatives to stop the violence. Eventually, the peace meeting organised by the Indonesian government in February 2002 in Malino, South Sulawesi, put an official end to the conflict, or at least to mass violence. The religious borderlines dissolved only gradually. After the conflict, local actors in the Moluccas hope to build up sustainable peace through the revival and/or strengthening of traditions, traditional leaders, structures and customary law that are supposed to overcome religious differences and enable sustainable peace and a harmonious living together. The *raja* as traditional leaders and potential mediators play a central role here.

The new national autonomy law gives such local tendencies legal support. In the explanations to law No. 32/2004 concerning the village level it is stated that diversity (*keragaman*) is to be acknowledged, that villages should be returned their original autonomy (*otonomi asli*), that they should be responsible for and take care of the concerns and interests of the local population in accordance with their ancestry (*asal usul*) and traditions (*adat istiadat*), that they should be allowed to rename the villages and the village heads according to their traditions (that is rename them *negeri* in place of *desa* or *raja* in place of *kepala desa* in the Central Moluccas), and to rename to *saniri* (in the Central Moluccan case) and restructure

[20] See, for example: Aditjondro 2001; K von Benda-Beckmann 2004; Bertrand 2002; Bräuchler 2003, 2005; Human Rights Watch 1999; International Crisis Group 2000, 2002; Klinken 2001b, 2007a; Pannell (ed.) 2003; Schulze 2002; Spyer 2002. This brief treatment, of course, does not do justice to the complexity of the conflict.

the village parliaments.[21] Article 203(3) of UU 32/2004 is dedicated to the village head election and stipulates that such "elections in a specific law community [*kesatuan masyarakat hukum*] take place according to its traditional rights [*hak tradisionalnya*] as long as they are still alive"; the respective adat law has to be specified in a Regional Regulation (Perda), guided by a Government Regulation. As Bedner and Huis judge, "an important avenue for indigenous communities to implement their own system is opened up, but it remains under the control of the government" (Bedner and Huis 2008: 173).

In the Moluccas, for a long time crippled by the violent conflict, a handful of actors – mainly jurists from the state university in Ambon (Universitas Pattimura) – finally catalysed the initiation of the process and tried to negotiate draft versions for the regional regulations concerning the decentralisation law, in cooperation with some *raja* from Ambon island. This led to the passing of the provincial *negeri* regulation in 2005 and the district regulation for the Central Moluccas in 2006: *Peraturan Daerah Provinsi Maluku Nomor 14 Tahun 2005 tentang Penetapan Kembali Negeri Sebagai Kesatuan Masyarakat Hukum Adat Dalam Wilayah Pemerintahan Provinsi Maluku* (Perda No. 14/2005 of the Moluccan Province about the Return to the negeri as adat law community in the territory of the Government of the Province of Maluku – in the following PerdaP 14/2005) and *Peraturan Daerah Kabupaten Maluku Tengah Nomor 1 Tahun 2006 tentang Negeri* (Perda No. 1/2006 of the Central Moluccan District about the Negeri – in the following PerdaK 1/2006), an umbrella Perda (*Perda payung*) that has been further specified in various sub-Perdas.[22] After PerdaP 14/2005 had been passed, the government of the Central Moluccan District hired a team (at home in various disciplines such as law, anthropology, agriculture and fishery) headed by a retired Ambonese professor of law. Based on their ethnographic knowledge of the area the team drafted PerdaK 1/2006 and 14 other Perdas in order to further elaborate the first.[23] The regulations cover issues such as the election of the *raja*, the functioning

[21] See the following explanations to UU 32/2004: General Explanations (*Penjelasan Umum*), section I, No. 10 (*Desa*), and explanations to the village chapter No. XI and to article 202 (1).

[22] By 2008 the Village Perdas for the other districts in the Moluccan province had not been passed yet (although for some of them drafts had already existed).

[23] Interestingly, when asked how such a huge variety of adat communities and ethnic groups can be subsumed under one provincial or district Perda that is concerned with local adat, the team head refers to van Vollenhoven who had, at the beginning of the 20th century, divided up Indonesia into 19 adat law areas

of village governments, *negeri* and financial matters and the set-up of the *saniri*. They were introduced and advertised in a meeting with Central Moluccan *raja*, who where then supposed to evaluate them. After villages have been familiarised with the Perda Kabupaten by the team, it is the village representatives' turn to formulate the Perda Negeri, that is to translate the Perda Kabupaten into the local context and elaborate it according to local adat. This will be task of the *saniri*. What local actors in the Moluccas such as the Perda team have to do is a rather difficult balancing act and the most critical level will be the Perda Negeri, since this is expected to be the most detailed one.

Generally, large parts of the Moluccan population on all levels seem to be very enthusiastic about the revitalisation prospects, about the fact that they are granted the collective right to return to their culture, and cultural self-determination which enables people "to exercise control over their own institutions, ways of life and economic development and to maintain and develop their identities, languages and religions, within the framework of the States in which they live" (ILO 169, preamble). The conflict background is an important reason for that (see, for example, Bräuchler 2009a, 2009b). In the Moluccas, adat people often claim that the return to a society determined by adat means the return to a civilised, orderly society (*beradab*), which was almost lost due to the developments of recent decades (*biadab*). As Tania Li argues, "to invoke adat is to claim purity and authenticity for one's cause" (Li 2007: 337). Many actors in the revival process in the Moluccas, be they NGOs, *raja* or other adat figures, try to give the impression that they want to revive an authentic, coherent and autonomous culture or a 'harmonious past'. Thus they aim to meet the requirements of the law and legitimise their claims. In the case of the *raja*, these are claims of leadership; in the case of NGOs, they are often the claims of an international human rights community.

What Adat?

Given the quite turbulent past, one needs to ask what adat it is that current revival activists actually refer to? Which traditions do they want to go back to and how 'traditional' are these? This illustrates one of the earlier mentioned central

(*adatrechtskringen*) – one of them consisting of the islands now constituting the Moluccan province – and argued that each one of them had certain key cultural elements.

problems with notions of 'cultural rights': are they premised on fixed ideals of culture and, importantly, who does the fixing and what are the power dynamics at work? The same issues emerge in other regions of Indonesia, such as in Minangkabau, where there is much discussion about

> to what type of *nagari* one should go back, how the representatives of the village parliament are to be chosen, what the role of the Village Adat Council will be and to what extent rights to village land (*ulayat*) are to be recognised and revitalised and who will hold them (F and K von Benda-Beckmann 2001: 16).

Refining UU 22/1999, UU 32/2004 gives villages a choice and differentiates between genealogical and administrative villages (*desa geneologis* and *desa administratif*):[24] The formers' population is supposed to still have a common history and adat so that they can make the claims just mentioned. Villages with a very heterogeneous population are declared to be administrative villages (with exceptions), as are those that were founded through the division of a village or for transmigrants and which therefore have no adat territory.[25] These villages then can still use the more 'neutral' uniform system introduced by UU 5/1979. In principle it is the village population's choice, how they will declare their village, but the final ratification is made by the district parliament. The question immediately arising out of the differentiation of genealogical and administrative villages is the question of how to determine which village is a *negeri adat*, that is an adat or, in the law's terminology, a genealogical village. The main criteria listed in PerdaP 14/2005 (Article 5 and explanations) are that an adat community (*masyarakat adat*) is bound together by both genealogical and territorial ties and should still adhere to its adat law (*hukum adat*). It must still inhabit its traditional territory (*wilayah petuanan*), and adat institutions such as the *raja* and the traditional village council (*saniri negeri*), as well as adat symbols such as the traditional community hall (*baileo*), must still be in place. This essentially is repeated in the *negeri* definition in chapter 1 of PerdaK 1/2006. In the explanations it emphasises again that all needs to be based on ancestry (*asal usul*) and local customs (*adat istiadat*) as a

[24] See General Explanations (*Penjelasan Umum*) of UU 32/2004, Section I, No. 10 (Desa).

[25] Depending on the adat community's lobby, there are exceptions to this rule such as Batumerah in Ambon town that was declared to be *negeri adat* although the majority of its population are migrants.

form of authority based on original autonomy (*otonomi asli*). At the same time, however, it is stressed that the adat community needs to be acknowledged and respected by the Government of the Unitary Republic of Indonesia and that the way it runs its governmental affairs has to be in line with national law (see chapter 1 and § 2 in chapter 2).

Not only because of this latter restriction, all this is quite problematic. What is "adat" is defined by those drafting the various regulations, and is heavily influenced by their background and their knowledge. Certain adat elements are inserted into local government regulations, which is, of course, far from a revial of adat in a holistic sense, but rather a selective reconstruction. However, the re-creation of holism is rather illusionary anyway, since it sets modernity apart from tradition. Modernity is not opposed to tradition, but, as in Indonesia, rather provides people with the means to revive their traditions, traditional structures and values as well as customary law. As the contributions to a special journal issue on *The revitalisation of tradition* illustrate, each of these recent revival processes - be it in Asia, Latin America or Africa - is based on complex negotiation processes. These oscillate between the selection of traditional elements from 'the past' and their use or instrumentalisation as future-oriented strategies (Bräuchler and Widlok 2007).

In addition and as mentioned above, forced 'cultural change' (induced by colonial and neo-colonial forces) is not taken into account by the law and the rather static notion of culture used is reminiscent of that which is criticised in connection with the grant of collective (human) rights. Just as the existence of such adat symbols, for example, does not necessarily mean that adat and adat values still determine the village people's life, their non-existence does not have to imply the absence of adat. Fixing local traditions in governmental regulations, a dilemma emerges that occurs whenever flexible and oral traditions and traditional law have to be written down or codified. The people involved in putting together the Perda on the various levels face the same predicament as van Vollenhoven and his colleagues almost a hundred years ago: the problem of codifying oral traditions and, at the same time, preserving their flexibility. What van Vollenhoven had suggested back then, is to abrogate each adat codification automatically after ten or fifteen years "in order to force the administration continuously to adapt the adat regulations to new developments and changed circumstances in native society" (Fasseur 2007: 58). Accordingly, today the Perda team propagates a notion of adat that needs to be open to development and social engineering and allow for variation and flexibility. Its head considers it to be dangerous to take the preservation of flexibility as an excuse not to write down adat and thus deprive the Moluccans of their unique chance; codification would also prevent the younger generation from forgetting their traditions.

Who are the Raja and how are they Legitimised?

Although adat is not all about *raja* and *negeri,* these are in the centre of current revival activities. They are key issues which are important as the starting-point of a long revival process where many questions still need to be answered. The *raja* are the heads of the local adat system and at the same time part of the national government system, which makes their position very influential. Promoters of the revival process see them as moral forces and means of integration and thus as key figures in the reconciliation and peace process as well as in the decentralisation and revival discourse (for more details see Bräuchler 2011). People in the villages have to collect proof not only of their status as an adat village, but also for the legitimation of *raja* candidates. Article 3 of PerdaK 1/2006 specifies that a *negeri* is led by a village head with the title *raja* or another name that is in line with local custom, customary law and culture (clause 1). It goes on to stipulate that a certain lineage (*matarumah/keturunan*) is entitled to the position of *negeri* head and that it is not to be transferred to another party, unless this is decided in a deliberative meeting (*musyawarah*) of the entitled lineage with the village council (*saniri negeri*) (clause 2).[26] As outlined in the explanations to article 3(2) such an exception would be made if the entitled lineage became extinct, if the entitled person is physically or mentally disabled in such a way that (s)he cannot fulfil the required tasks, or if the person concerned, for example, is prone to drink or gamble, or does not fulfil the legal requirements (such as age and education). In this way a certain kind of flexibility has been explicitly incorporated. If there is only one candidate who fulfils all the legal and adat requirements, s/he will be appointed; if there are two or more, s/he will be elected (article 6(1)). No advice is given, however, on how to deal with the tumultuous past of some *raja* lineages.

[26] PerdaK 1/2006, § 3 (1): *Negeri dipimpin oleh seorang Kepala Pemerintah Negeri dengan gelar Raja atau disebut dengan nama lain sesuai adat istiadat, hukum adat dan budaya setempat; (2) Jabatan Kepala Pemerintahan Negeri merupakan hak dari matarumah/keturunan tertentu berdasarkan garis keturunan lurus dan tidak dapat dialihkan kepada pihak lain, kecuali dalam hal-hal khusus yang ditetapkan berdasarkan hasil musyawarah matarumah/keturunan yang berhak bersama Saniri Negeri.*

A related question is, who may claim to speak for 'a culture', who constructs this uniform image that enables the community to claim their rights, and out of which interests and with what legitimation. It will always be certain spokespersons of a village, certain adat figures or the *raja* who will try to provide proof to the evaluators. Since the *raja* were only recently reinstalled as village heads, there are still many issues to be solved. Unlike the *kepala desa*, who has been in charge since the law on village unification (UU 5/1979) and who was democratically elected (at least on paper, although in fact often appointed by the central government), the *raja* is a hereditary position. Their reinstallation triggered discussions on democracy issues and who is actually allowed to step into these revived positions - questions of genealogy and descent, but also of political principle. But in most cases it is also a question of power: struggles between those who have been in power before colonial times and those in power during that period, between those elected as village heads (*kepala desa*) when UU 5/1979 was in use and those who now want to reclaim their hereditary positions (for Minangkabau compare F and K von Benda-Beckmann 2001: 21). In many places in the Central Moluccas, *raja* installation ceremonies that have been postponed for periods because of the conflict, are now due. Different attempts to (re)interpret history in order to determine who and which lineage is actually entitled to be *raja* can lead to the splitting of whole villages or cause *raja* candidates to go to court to fight for their alleged rights, as happened in Haria (Saparua island). On the other hand, *raja* installation ceremonies also became important peace events, where the revival of reconciliatory adat, such as *pela*, is put very much into the forefront, and *raja* are celebrated as mediators and peace keepers. (For more details and examples see Bräuchler 2009a.)

What took place in Hulaliu, a village on Haruku Island, can be taken as a rather dramatic instance of what may happen if deliberation about the problematic and ambivalent nature of the *raja* issue does not take place among all sides involved, that is, policy makers, power holders and the common people.[27] In July 2006, the *raja* of Hulaliu was killed in his own village as a result of internal village disputes. He had been living in Ambon city for many years, but belonged to the proper lineage, was educated and experienced, and was therefore asked to return to his

[27] Just as in Minangkabau, the common village population felt less involved in the deliberation and decision making process and, as Franz and Keebet von Benda-Beckmann put it, "they have cynical views about the political rhetoric which is so strongly emphasising adat values and the 'bottom-up' character of the political process" (F and K von Benda-Beckmann 2001: 22).

village and become *raja* in 2003.[28] One of the issues in the murder was the (seemingly) authoritarian way in which the new *raja* had revived adat, in particular adat sanctions.[29] This extreme case gives expression to the rather tense political situation in many villages in the decentralisation era. It is not only a matter of power struggles, but also a symptom of another phenomenon that impedes the re-empowerment of the *raja*. Respect for and the influence of many Central Moluccan *raja* as moral authorities has declined enormously during the last decades, especially among the younger generation, whether because of the influence of UU 5/1979 or because of urbanisation and modernisation processes. This decline affects issues ranging from smaller issues such as villagers no longer paying proper respect by bowing when the *raja* passes by, to quite dramatic cases such as that in Hulaliu.

Another contentious issue in the struggle for power is article 23(b) of PerdaK 1/2006, which prohibits the *raja* from acting as head of the village council (*saniri negeri*), in order to prevent excessive accumulation of power. According to a lecturer in law at Pattimura University, who was involved in drafting and introducing the district Perdas concerning the *negeri*, almost two thirds of the *raja* agreed with this stipulation in 2007. Nevertheless, this means that a third did not, and showed either overt or indirect resistance. Also there are certain sub-districts where at least half of the *raja* were not ready to accept the clause, that is a sharp break with the past, in UU 5/1979 requiring the village head to be head of the village parliament (*Lembaga Musyawarah Desa*), thus making him an influential representative of the central government on the village level. According to earlier research, the *raja* also used to be the head of the village council before UU 5/1979

---

[28] A similar trend was identified by Franz and Keebet von Benda-Beckmann in West Sumatra in the decentralisation era:

> Many (often retired) migrants, who had lost interest in village affairs, have taken a renewed and active interest in their village or origin. Some have taken on office as adat leader, as official advisor, or even as mayor. Wearing several hats at the same time, neither a real insider nor a real outsider, they contribute to the construction of Minangkabau identity and to the more mundane concerns of village administration and politics (F and K von Benda-Beckmann 2007a: 437-438).

[29] There were other issues involved as well, but further analysis would go beyond the scope of this paper.

(Bartels 1994: 308; Cooley 1987: 238), but, as adat elders in a variety of central Moluccan villages affirmed to me, the *raja* was not able then to make any decision without the approval of the *saniri*.

To add to these difficulties, many villages experienced a governmental vacuum because of the coincidence of the Moluccan conflict with the transition period. Some villages had temporary village heads (*penjabat*) for several years, and, when the *raja* had been finally installed but no governmental body formed, there were tendencies in some villages for the *raja* to became autocrats. Often these *raja* claim that this is not their fault, since they were still waiting for a Perda.[30] But in fact the new law gives the villages quite considerable space to decide for themselves. Of course, it is not only passivity that is to be blamed, but also a matter of the familiarisation with and popularisation of the new legislation by the government.

Local Approaches to the Problem: Reconstructing Adat in Honitetu[31]

There are local approaches to solving internal conflicts over some of these matters and to (re)building old government structures anew. Honitetu village in Western Seram is an interesting example and also shows how 'translators' come into the scene, acting as "knowledge brokers between culturally distinct social worlds" (Merry 2005: 2), helping to localise human rights discourses as well as national legislation, and facilitating the transition period. In the Moluccas, the reconstruction of history and genealogy is a crucial element in the rhetoric of the revival era, and the basis for the construction anew of an old collective identity and the restoration of former power structures (for Minangkabau compare F and K von Benda-Beckmann 2001). Since the early 1990s people in Honitetu have been thinking about reviving adat and traditions in order to prevent further moral

[30] While the Perda Kabupaten Maluku Tengah concerning the *Negeri* was passed relatively quickly in 2006 (see above), most of the other districts in 2008 were still waiting for the regulations to be passed by the regional parliaments. Passing, of course, does not yet mean implementation, and all Perda Kabupaten still need to be 'translated' into village regulations.

[31] Since the recent separation of Western Seram (Seram Bagian Barat, SBB) from Kabupaten Maluku Tengah (*pemekaran*), Honitetu is now part of this new kabupaten from an administrative point of view. The Perda Negeri for SBB had still not been passed by 2008.

'degeneracy'; the lack of sources and the existing variety of versions of history posed major problems. Revival activists in Honitetu have therefore set up three teams of adat functionaries, whose task is to undertake research in the field of culture (*budaya dan kesenian* – mainly material culture and arts), tradition and customary law (*adat-istiadat*) and history (*sejarah*). These efforts are viewed as opening up the possibility for the creation of a consistent version of history, which all can identify with. This is a process not without its problems, since questions of representation and authority play a role, as do also the choice of mechanisms to familiarise villagers with the results.

Crucial to current revival processes is the re-establishment of traditional institutions and symbols, such as the *raja*, the *saniri* and the *baileo*. These efforts of the Honitetu people were facilitated by a local NGO, which entered the area in order to support the village in the matter of logging licences in their territory which the central government had illegally given to an external company without seeking the villagers' permission. The NGO in question is Baileo (in connection with Humanum), which was set up in Ambon in 1993 and has been engaged in adat matters since then.[32] It is one of the few long-lasting and experienced NGOs in the Moluccas, which has served as 'translator' and broker in human rights issues and national legislation in many cases. These brokers also exert their influence on the people they work with, for instance, with their perceptions of 'tradition'. One example occurred in the production of a video about the ceremonial reconstruction process of the *baileo* in Honitetu. The NGO filmmaker complained about people involved not wearing traditional village dresses such as the loincloth, which is rarely, if ever, worn today, but colourful political party shirts or military-style clothes, that is, the clothes of the 'enemy'. One reason for this attitude is that these brokers are torn between two sides: the interest of local populations and lived culture, and the international donors, who are interested in specific topics and who often tend to essentialise culture (see above and also Merry 2005: 15).

Baileo/Humanum also facilitated the reinstallation procedure of the *raja* in Honitetu. In close cooperation with adat representatives and young people from Honitetu enthusiastic to learn more about adat, it set up meetings and helped prepare documents, but generally tried not to influence the deliberation and decision process as such. The process lasted several years, during which

[32] I would like to thank the Baileo/Humanum crew, who drew my attention to this particular case, for their cooperativeness and their friendship.

representatives and adat functionaries of the two groups of the *raja* candidates often met, discussing history and genealogies, reflecting on adat procedures and asking the candidates to deliver proof of the legitimacy of their candidacies. Following these procedures, a document was released in July 2006 by the *saniri negeri* Honitetu, in which finally one of the candidates was declared the legitimate descendant. However, the decision was then revoked, since the opposition in the village was still too strong. Up to 2008 the situation had not been regularised, and the *penjabat* was still in charge. Depending on one's point of view, this can be interpreted either as a positive example of practised (revived) village democracy or, as Franz von Benda-Beckmann has put it, as "business as usual" (personal communication November 2010). Because of the turbulent past of most villages in Maluku and the complex and ambivalent history of the role of the *raja* described above, time-consuming discussions and contests between various lineages who claim to be entitled to the *raja* post have always been on the agenda.

The Exclusion of Migrants

Migrants, who are still a minority in Honitetu, further complicate the situation. As in most adat villages, immigrants are welcome as long as they accept local adat, follow its rules and do not carry out their own adat ceremonies in public.[33] They are not included in the current local research processes and they cannot be nominated as *raja* candidates. This makes the revival efforts in Honitetu, although they are based on a thorough deliberation process, exclusive and problematic. These 'others', that is, people who have no place in the adat structure of the village they live in, are understandably the main critics of the current revival processes (for Minangkabau see F and K von Benda-Beckmann 2009: 312-313). The collective cultural rights granted to one group (based on national and international law) severely restrict the rights of others not belonging to this adat group and thus their rights as equal citizens of Indonesia and their human right to equal treatment. In Indonesia, as Bourchier argues, adat revival "sharpens distinctions between cultural insiders and outsiders, increasing the potential for horizontal conflict and violence" (Bourchier 2007: 124; compare also Kuper 2003:

[33] This is supported by jurists involved in drafting the Perda concerning the village reforms. According to one of them this is not a problem, since those migrants are interested only in territorial questions, not genealogical ties. But, one might object, *negeri* are not only bound by genealogical ties, but also by territorial relations that can easily come into conflict with the migrants' land claims.

395). In order to solve the migrant problem, the part of Honitetu where most migrants live (Uraur) has been officially declared to be an independent administrative village, a solution that not all people in Honitetu, especially adat figures, approve. However, when it comes to adat matters such as communal land and marriage sanctions, Uraur is still under the authority of Honitetu. Another migrant issue not solved yet in Honitetu concerns the occupants of the Muslim enclave who migrated to the area in the 1970s from Haruku island following a government scheme. These Muslims have fled predominantly Christian Honitetu during the recent violence and have not returned yet. Debates about whether Honitetu Christians want to receive them back and whether the refugees actually want to return were still ongoing in 2008.

Another category of migrants more gravely affected by the Moluccan conflict were those from outside the area, most prominently the so-called BBM, that is people from Bugis, Buton and Makassar (South Sulawesi). Although some of those families had settled in the Moluccas several generations ago, many of them fled during the first days of the Moluccan conflict. At that time it still looked as if the violence was mostly directed towards them, as has been the case in such places as Kalimantan, where the indigenous Dayak were fighting and expelling Madurese migrants (see, for example, Davidson 2008). The BBM, although Muslim, were never fully integrated into Moluccan Muslim society. The Butonese, as Franz and Keebet von Benda-Beckmann's research in Hila village (Ambon island) illustrates, are not considered citizens in adat terms and do not or only marginally participate in village government:

> Being second class village citizens, they could acquire only temporary rights to agricultural land and cash tree cultivation and were entirely dependent on Ambonese owners for access to land and trees (F and K von Benda-Beckmann 2007b: 23; see also F and K von Benda-Beckmann 1998).

Even during the New Order, when all citizens (so long as their age and education were appropriate) should have had equal rights to become *raja* candidates, for example, adat principles proved to be stronger in Hila, just as in many other Moluccan villages (F von Benda-Beckmann 1990: 31). Ambonese villagers, as Franz von Benda-Beckmann argued,

> use their own law in order to shield themselves against the claims of the state for more extended control over natural and human resources. Simultaneously, Ambonese adat is maintained to

> rationalize and justify relations of dominance and oppression of the immigrant Butonese (F von Benda-Beckmann 1990: 39-40).

This can easily be transferred to the post-Suharto situation. In the post-conflict era, the immigrants' situation seems to be even more precarious, as Jeroen Adam's study shows. Whereas many went back to Sulawesi triggered by the violence, a considerable part remained on Ambon (Adam 2009: 184).[34] Because of their flight and relocation, oral sharecropping arrangements, which were the only way for non-adat-people to get access to land, ceased to be in force, thus robbing them of their means of subsistence and further increasing their social vulnerability. (For a more extensive report on the situation of selected Butonese settlements on Ambon see Adam 2009.) Alternative income is difficult to find, since "the informal economy in urban and peri-urban regions on the island of Ambon is already overcrowded" and "the squatting of arable land by displaced Butonese communities poses a problem" in many places on post-conflict Ambon (Adam 2009: 177, 185). This hopeless situation pushes some Butonese to become active and assert their right to be recognized "as real Moluccans with the same rights" (Adam 2009: 186). To emphasise this, as Adam argues, in 2005 they renamed a Butonese organisation in Ambon, which had been called *Badan Keturunan Masyarakat Sulawesi Tengara* (Committee of the Descendants of Southeast Sulawesi Society) *Badan Keturunan Masyarakat Maluku – Sulawesi Tenggara* (Committee of the Descendants of Moluccan Society – Southeast Sulawesi). Both stronger political representation and an increasing say in resource management are central to their struggle (Adam 2009: 185-186). Although the power of such organisations is still limited, "it is an undeniable fact that resentment among many ethnic Butonese has sharply increased since the conflict, and will be a factor to be reckoned with in the future" (Adam 2009: 186). For these various reasons, the migrant issue needs to be urgently dealt with in the current decentralisation and revitalisation process, in which arguments for the observance of international standards of democracy and human rights figure so prominently.

Cultural Flexibility, Human Rights and Legal Pluralism

Given the many downsides of the adat revival in the Moluccas, an unconditional

[34] In the first phase of the violence approximately 160.000 Butonese fled to Buton (Palmer 2004: 89), their "land of origin", although many of them grew up on Ambon and had never been there before.

revival would rather be counterproductive, as shown throughout this article. I would argue that it is crucial to preserve the flexibility of adat in order to adapt it to changing political, social and economic circumstances and to accommodate all people living in such territories, both cultural insiders and outsiders. I therefore end this contribution with reflections on the preservation of cultural flexibility and the challenges arising in a situation where a grant of the right to culture collides with a Western understanding of democracy. These are issues that need urgent attention by policy makers and researchers.[35]

Both scholars and activists, as Cowan et al. argue, should start seeing

> cultural change as potentially positive, as well as inevitable ... An endangered 'culture' is perceived as a pre-existing given which must be defended, rather than as something creatively reworked during struggles to actualise rights (Cowan et al. 2001b: 19).

It helps to call to mind again, that 'traditional' models such as the *negeri* so many revival activists refer to are not eternal concepts, but rather recent constructions. Change, as one of the founders of the Ambonese NGO Hualopu argues, has to be included in all thoughts about revitalisation and future planning, including the use of traditional mechanisms for peace. Customary law, just as human rights, has to be seen as a social construct born out of and developed in a specific socio-historic context. Customary law in post-colonial societies, which people refer to or want to revitalise nowadays, is not an unchanging heritage to be rediscovered from the pre-colonial past, but something that was (partly) constructed, if not invented in the colonial period through the interaction of the colonial powers with the local contexts (see, for example, K von Benda-Beckmann 2007). Revitalisation therefore should not be confused with the literal 'revival of the past'. Instead it should be seen as a process of taking up traditional principles, developing them further, and adapting them to the people's needs and current circumstances.

[35] Boundaries are blurred. As Otto and Pedersen argue:

> [I]t is not necessary to be a consultant anthropologist in order to become caught up in moral dilemmas and political conflicts when writing about traditions ... Anthropologists get entangled in politics and morality ... because ... the subject matter of anthropology is inherently political, and because researchers cannot avoid being actors in the world they investigate (Otto and Pedersen 2005: 42).

To close the circle, I will now come back to the problematic relationship between collective human rights or the right to culture, and Western notions of democracy that seem to prevail among observers of the decentralisation process in Indonesia. How can the idea of a democratically elected village head and parliament be reconciled with the idea of the *raja* as a hereditary position as implied in the cultural revival process? This is an even more pressing issue, since the Moluccan population seems to be divided over the question as to how far the revival of tradition should go: as to whether it should mainly imply a rather folkloristic revival or whether political institutions and procedures should be reintroduced or re-empowered as well. In the former case advocates of a holistic revival fear the further dilution of local adat; in the latter case the advocates of democratic elections fear the return of feudalism and autocratic-genealogical structures, where individual performance and education as selection criteria come second. But they also fear that adat might be instrumentalised to achieve political goals as in the *putra daerah* cases mentioned earlier.

In order to preserve flexibility and make adat mechanisms fit post-conflict requirements, social engineering, that is, the planned adaptation to current circumstances, has been suggested by a number of people (see above). In reaction to the current omnipresence of democratisation discourses, adat functionaries in Moluccan villages often claim that democracy is already embedded in their adat system, and that their decision-making processes, based on deliberation and consensus (as in the Honitetu case), are even more democratic than the 'Western' idea of the concept (for Minangkabau see F and K von Benda-Beckmann 2007a: 436). Fauzi and Zakaria point to the ambiguity of the current revitalisation processes and give some recommendations in their paper on 'Democratizing Decentralization: Local Initiatives from Indonesia' (Fauzi and Zakaria 2002). They praise the new possibilities provided by the new autonomy law that explicitly recognises the village as "a legal community that possesses its own 'original rights', norms and relations" and greatly reduces "the distance between communities and policy-makers" (Fauzi and Zakaria 2002: 3). But they also emphasize that caution is needed so that the inclusion of local communities in the political process will not "end up creating a situation wherein all of the shortcomings of the prior centralized system are merely replicated on a smaller scale by local government authorities" (Fauzi and Zakaria 2002: 9). Concerning the reintroduction of clan-based village governments, the authors argue that democratic principles (in a Western sense?) still have to be an imperative prerequisite and a compromise has to be found, which presents quite a challenge to adat leaders. Similarly, Merry warns us that human rights programs should be appropriated and translated into local context, but not fully indigenised:

> To blend completely with the surrounding social worlds is to lose the radical possibilities of human rights. It is the unfamiliarity of these ideas that makes them effective in breaking old modes of thought, for example, denaturalising male privilege to use violence against women as a form of discipline (Merry 2006: 178).

Human rights must not be deconstructed by culturally determined arguments. One could conclude from this argumentation that we have to refrain both from a concept of culture as an unchangeable object and from a misunderstood cultural relativism that releases people from any responsibilities, and which is not tolerable any more in a globalised world. This puts anthropologists researching such issues in a difficult situation, since it is their subjects of study that prioritise identity and culture and a specific way of representing it (compare also Guenther et al. 2006: 18).

Despite all objections and despite the serious challenges discussed here, the new law on decentralisation still provides a unique and (in Indonesia) unprecedented opportunity for more self-determination on the local level.[36] Although it is not my objective to formulate detailed policy and implementation guidelines, I nonetheless hope that this article has raised a number of questions and expressed various caveats that urgently need to be taken into account by whoever is involved in that. It is important to take all levels into account: the international, the national, the regional and the local. Although all of them are (seemingly) concerned with the local (with regard to decentralisation, for example), the knowledge about it, the context and the interests involved vary extensively. As argued by Wilson and Freeman human rights set only a minimal standard and do not provide the means to solve all moral, political and economic problems of our times (Freeman 2000: 56; Wilson 2006: 82). What is still necessary is a dialogue on and between all levels, which involves all interest groups, and a lot of work on the ground. In his edited volume on *Human Rights in Cross-Cultural Perspectives* An-Na'im strives to explore "the possibilities of cultural reinterpretation and reconstruction through *internal cultural discourse and cross-cultural dialogue*, as a means to enhancing the universal legitimacy of human rights" (An-Na'im 1992: 3). For the Moluccan

[36] Analogously, Widlok warns against a rash disposal of the concept of indigeneity, as suggested by Kuper, when certain elites instrumentalise indigenous rights for their advantage at the expense of the indigenous people, since this could rather aggravate the latter's situation (Kuper 2003; Widlok 2007).

case of revitalisation and reconciliation this means internal dialogue in local communities such as in Honitetu, and also dialogue between these communities and 'the others' and with the Moluccan society at large. It also means that local discourses can be influenced externally by international discourses, such as that on human rights, through mediators, brokers and translators such as NGOs. In the future, the way 'the others' (migrants from inside and outside the Moluccas) are dealt with, perceived and integrated into reconstructed local communities and systems will significantly influence the success of the decentralisation and democratisation project. They not only have to be tolerated, but they have to be given a participatory role in the 'traditional' system. A successful dialogue has to guarantee that everybody gets her/his say in the revitalisation and reconciliation process, and the negotiations between individual and collective rights and the legal systems involved - international human rights, state law and local customary law. This would enable us to translate human rights into cultural contexts without taking the risk of restricting 'other' people's rights. The universality of human rights

> should be seen as a *product of a process* rather than as an established 'given' concept and specific predetermined normative content to be discovered or proclaimed through international declarations and rendered legally binding through treaties (An-Na'im 2003: 2).

Ethnographic methods allow social anthropologists to conduct in-depth studies on the local level and analyse its interlinkage with 'the others' and its embeddedness in the larger context. This knowledge can make major contributions to developing strategies for integrating collective and individual human rights and for fostering a revival of tradition that is integrative rather than exclusivist.

References

ACCIAIOLI, Greg
2001 'Grounds of Conflict, Idioms of Harmony: Custom, Religion, and Nationalism in Violence Avoidance at the Lindu Plain, Central Sulawesi.' *Indonesia* 72 (October 2001): 81-114.

ADAM, Jeroen
2009 'Communal Violence, Forced Migration and Social Change on the Island of Ambon, Indonesia.' [PhD dissertation, Ghent University].

ADITJONDRO, George Junus
2001 'Guns, Pamphlets and Handie-Talkies: How the military exploited local ethno-religious tensions in Maluku to preserve their political and economic privileges.' Pp. 100-128 in Ingrid Wessel and Georgia Wimhöfer (eds.), *Violence in Indonesia*. Hamburg: Abera-Verlag.
ANDAYA, Leonard Y.
1993 *The World of Maluku. Eastern Indonesia in the Early Modern Period*. Honolulu: University of Hawaii Press.
AN-NA'IM, Abdullahi A.
1992 'Introduction.' Pp. 1-16 in Abdullahi Ahmed An-Na'im (ed.), *Human Rights in Cross-Cultural Perspectives: A Quest for Consensus*. Philadelphia: University of Pennsylvania Press.
2003 'Introduction: "Area Expressions" and the Universality of Human Rights: Mediating a Contingent Relationship.' Pp. 1-21 in: David P. Forsythe and Patrice C. McMahon (eds.), *Human Rights and Diversity: Area Studies Revisited*. Lincoln/London: University of Nebraska Press.
ARAGON, Lorraine V.
2001 'Communal Violence in Poso, Central Sulawesi: Where People Eat Fish and Fish Eat People.' *Indonesia* 72 (October 2001): 45-79.
ASPINALL, Edward and Greg FEALY
2003 *Local Power and Politics in Indonesia: Decentralisation and Democratisation*. Singapore: Institute of Southeast Asian Studies.
BACH, Jan-Michael
2003 *Dezentralisierung und Lokalregierung in Indonesien seit 1998: Der Fall Riau*. Studien zur Volkswirtschaft des Vorderen Orients 11. Münster: LIT.
BADAN PUSAT STATISTIK PROPINSI MALUKU
2007 *Maluku Dalam Angka 2007 (Maluku in Figures 2007)*. Ambon.
BARNARD, Alan
2006 'Kalahari revisionism, Vienna and the "indigenous peoples" debate.' *Social Anthropology* 14(1): 1-16.
BARTELS, Dieter
1977 *Guarding the Invisible Mountain: Intervillage Alliances, Religious Syncretism and Ethnic Identity among Ambonese Christians and Moslems in the Moluccas*. Ithaca: Cornell University.
1994 *In de Schaduw van de Berg Nunusaku: Een Cultuur-historische Verhandeling over de Bevolking van de Midden-Molukken*. Utrecht: Landelijk Steunpunt Educatie Molukkers (LSEM).
2003 'Your God Is No Longer Mine: Moslem-Christian Fratricide in the Central Moluccas (Indonesia) After a Half-Millennium of Tolerant Co-

Existence and Ethnic Unity.' Pp. 128-153 in Pannell (ed.).
BEDNER, Adriaan and Stijn van HUIS
2008 'The return of the native in Indonesian law: Indigenous communities in Indonesian legislation.' *Bijdragen tot de Taal-, Land- en Volkenkunde* 164(2/3): 165-193.
BENDA-BECKMANN, Franz von
1988 'Islamic Law and social security in an Ambonese village.' Pp. 339-365 in Franz and Keebet von Benda-Beckmann, E. Casino, F. Hirtz, G. R. Woodman and H. F. Zacher (eds.), *Between Kinship and the State. Social Security and Law in Developing Countries*. Dordrecht: Foris Publications.
1990 'Ambonese Adat as Jurisprudence of Insurgency and Oppression.' *Law & Anthropology. Internationales Jahrbuch für Rechtsanthropologie* 5: 25-42.
1999 'Multiple Legal Constructions of Socio-economic Spaces: Resource Management and Conflict in the Central Moluccas.' Pp. 131-158 in Michael Rösler and Tobias Wendl (eds.), *Frontiers and Borderlands. Anthropological Perspectives*. Frankfurt am Main: Peter Lang Verlag.
2009 'Human Rights, Cultural Relativism and Legal Pluralism: Towards a Two-dimensional Debate.' Pp. 115-134 in Franz von Benda-Beckmann, Keebet von Benda-Beckmann and Anne Griffiths (eds.), *The Power of Law in a Transnational World: Anthropological Enquiris*. New York/Oxford: Berghahn Books.
BENDA-BECKMANN, Franz von and Keebet von BENDA-BECKMANN
1998 'Where Structures Merge: State and Off-State Involvement in Rural Social Security on Ambon, Eastern Indonesia.' Pp. 143-180 in Sandra Pannell and Franz von Benda-Beckmann (eds.), *Old World Places, New World Problems: Exploring Issues of Resource Management in Eastern Indonesia*. Canberra: Centre for Resource and Environmental Studies, The Australian National University.
2001 'Recreating the *Nagari*: Decentralisation in West Sumatra.' Working Paper No. 31, Max Planck Institute for Social Anthropology, Halle/Saale.
2007a 'Ambivalent identities: Decentralization and Minangkabau political communties.' Pp. 417-442 in Henk Schulte Nordholt and Gerry van Klinken (eds.), *Renegotiating Boundaries: Local politics in post-Suharto Indonesia*. Leiden: KITLV Press.
2007b 'Social Security Between Past and Future: Introduction.' Pp. 1-24 in Franz von Benda-Beckmann and Keebet von Benda-Beckmann (eds.), *Social Security Between Past and Future: Ambonese Networks of Care and Support*. Münster: LIT.
2008 'Transforming traditions: Myths and stereotypes about traditional law in a globalizing world.' Paper presented at the EASA conference

'Experiencing Diversity and Mutuality', Ljubljana, Slovenia, 26-30 August 2008.

2009 'Recentralization and decentralization in West Sumatra.' Pp. 293-328 in Coen J.G. Holtzappel and Martin Ramstedt (eds.), *Decentralization and Regional Autonomy in Indonesia: Implementation and Challenges*. Singapore/Leiden: ISEAS/IIAS.

BENDA-BECKMANN, Keebet von

2004 'Law, Violence and Peace Making on the Island of Ambon.' Pp. 221-239 in Marie-Claire Foblets and Trutz von Trotha (eds.), *Healing the Wounds: Essays on the Reconstruction of Societies after War*. Oxford and Portland Oregon: Hart Publishing.

2007 'Law, Violence and Peace Making on the Island of Ambon.' Pp. 281-298 in Franz von Benda-Beckmann and Keebet von Benda-Beckmann (eds.), *Social Security Between Past and Future: Ambonese Networks of Care and Support*. Münster: LIT.

BERTRAND, Jacques

2002 'Legacies of the Authoritarian Past: Religious Violence in Indonesia's Moluccan Islands.' *Pacific Affairs* Spring 2002: 57-85.

BOURCHIER, David

2007 'The romance of adat in the Indonesian political imagination and the current revival.' Pp. 113-129 in Davidson and Henley (eds.).

BRÄUCHLER, Birgit

2003 'Cyberidentities at War: Religion, Identity, and the Internet in the Moluccan Conflict.' *Indonesia* 75: 123-151.

2005 *Cyberidentities at War: Der Molukkenkonflikt im Internet*. Bielefeld: transcript.

2007 'Ein Comeback der Tradition? Die Revitalisierung von Adat in Ostindonesien / A Comeback of Tradition? The Revitalisation of Adat in Eastern Indonesia.' *Zeitschrift für Ethnologie,* Special issue, Birgit Bräuchler and Thomas Widlok (eds.), *Die Revitalisierung von Tradition / The Revitalisation of Tradition* 132: 37-57.

2009a 'Cultural Solutions to Religious Conflicts? The Revival of Tradition in the Moluccas, Eastern Indonesia.' *Asian Journal of Social Sciences* 37(6): 872-891.

2009b 'Mobilising culture and tradition for peace: Reconciliation in the Moluccas.' Pp. 97-118 in Birgit Bräuchler (ed.), *Reconciling Indonesia: Grassroots agency for peace*. London/New York: Routledge.

2011 'Kings on Stage: Local Leadership in the Post-Suharto Moluccas.' *Asian Journal of Social Sciences* 39(2): 196-218.

BRÄUCHLER, Birgit and Thomas WIDLOK
2007 'Die Revitalisierung von Tradition: Im (Ver-)Handlungsfeld zwischen staatlichem und lokalem Recht / The revitalisation of tradition: Agency and negotiations between state law and local law.' *Zeitschrift für Ethnologie,* Special issue, Birgit Bräuchler and Thomas Widlok (eds.), *Die Revitalisierung von Tradition / The Revitalisation of Tradition* 132: 5-14.

BRUUN, Ole and Michael JACOBSEN
2000 'Introduction.' Pp. 1-20 in Michael Jacobsen and Ole Bruun (eds.), *Human Rights and Asian Values: Contesting National Identities and Cultural Representations in Asia*. Surrey: Curzon.

BUBANDT, Nils
2002 'Decentralisation, Conflict, and the New Politics of Tradition in North Maluku.' Pp. 114-127 in Kivimäki et al. (eds.).

BURNS, Peter
2004 *The Leiden Legacy: Concepts of Law in Indonesia*. Leiden: KITLV Press.
2007 'Custom, that is before all law.' Pp. 68-86 in Davidson and Henley (eds.).

CHAN, Joseph
2000 'Thick and Thin Accounts of Human Rights.' Pp. 59-74 in Michael Jacobsen and Ole Bruun (eds.), *Human Rights and Asian Values: Contesting National Identities and Cultural Representations in Asia*. Surrey: Curzon.

CHAUVEL, Richard
1990 *Nationalists, Soldiers and Separatists. The Ambonese Islands from Colonialism to Revolt, 1880-1950*. Verhandelingen van het Koninklijk Instituut voor Taal-, Land- en Volkenkunde 143. Leiden: KITLV Press.

CHRISTIE, Kenneth and Denny ROY
2001 *The Politics of Human Rights in East Asia*. London/Sterling,VA: Pluto Press.

COOLEY, Frank L.
1961 'Altar and Throne in Central Moluccan Societies: a study of the relationship between the institutions of religion and the institutions of local society undergoing rapid social change.' Dissertation presented to the Faculty of the Department of Religion Yale University. New Haven: Yale University.
1987 *Mimbar dan Takhta: Hubungan Lembaga-lembaga Keagamaan dan Pemerintahan di Maluku Tangah*. Jakarta: Pustaka Sinar Harapan.

COWAN, Jane K.
2001 'Ambiguities of an emancipatory discourse: the making of a Macedonian

minority in Greece.' Pp. 152-176 in Jane K. Cowan, Marie-Bénédicte Dembour and Richard A. Wilson (eds.), *Culture and Rights: Anthropological Perspectives*. Cambridge: Cambridge University Press.

2006 'Culture and Rights after *Culture and Rights*.' *American Anthropologist* 108(1): 9-24.

COWAN, Jane K., Marie-Bénédicte DEMBOUR and Richard A. WILSON

2001a 'Claiming cultural rights.' Pp. 149-151 in Jane K. Cowan, Marie-Bénédicte Dembour and Richard A. Wilson (eds.), *Culture and Rights: Anthropological Perspectives*. Cambridge: Cambridge University Press.

2001b 'Introduction.' Pp. 1-26 in Jane K. Cowan, Marie-Bénédicte Dembour and Richard A. Wilson (eds.), *Culture and Rights: Anthropological Perspectives*. Cambridge: Cambridge University Press.

DAVIDSON, Jamie S.

2007 'Culture and rights in ethnic violence.' Pp. 224-246 in Davidson and Henley (eds.).

2008 *From Rebellion to Riots: Collective Violence on Indonesian Borneo*. Madison Wisconsin: University of Wisconsin Press.

DAVIDSON, Jamie S. and David HENLEY (eds.)

2007 *The Revival of Tradition in Indonesian Politics: The deployment of adat from colonialism to indigenism*. London/New York: Routledge.

EYSINK, Simone

2006 'Human Rights between Europe and Southeast Asia.' *IIAS Newsletter* 41: 8-9.

FASSEUR, C.

2007 'Colonial Dilemma: Van Vollenhoven and the struggle between adat law and Western law in Indonesia.' Pp. 50-67 in Davidson and Henley (eds.).

FAUZI, Noer and R. Yando ZAKARIA

2002 'Democratizing Decentralization: Local Initiatives from Indonesia.' Paper presented at the 9th Biennial Conference of the International Association for the Study of Common Property, Victoria Falls, Zimbabwe. http://dlc.dlib.indiana.edu/archive/00000818/01/fauzin170502.pdf (accessed 7.11.2005).

FORSYTHE, David P. and Patrice C. McMAHON

2003 'Conclusion: Rights, Practices and "Area Studies".' Pp. 297-316 in David P. Forsythe and Patrice C. McMahon (eds.), *Human Rights and Diversity: Area Studies Revisited*. Lincoln/London: University of Nebraska Press.

FRAASSEN, Chris Frans van

1972 *Ambon-Rapport*, Doktoraalskriptie. Leiden: Stichting Werkgroep Studiereizen Ontwikkelingslanden.

FRAASSEN, Chris Frans van and Hans STRAVER
2002 *De Ambonse eilanden onder de VOC zoals opgetekend in De Ambonse Landbeschrijving (Georgius Everhardus Rumphius)*. Utrecht: Landelijk Steunpunt Educatie Molukkers.
FREEMAN, Michael
2000 'Universal Rights and Particular Cultures.' Pp. 43-58 in Michael Jacobsen and Ole Bruun (eds.), *Human Rights and Asian Values: Contesting National Identities and Cultural Representations in Asia*. Surrey: Curzon.
GELLNER, David N.
2001 'From group rights to individual rights and back: Nepalese struggles over culture and equality.' Pp. 177-200 in Jane K. Cowan, Marie-Bénédicte Dembour and Richard A. Wilson (eds.), *Culture and Rights: Anthropological Perspectives*. Cambridge: Cambridge University Press.
GUENTHER, Mathias, Justin KENRICK, Adam KUPER, Evie PLAICE, Trond THUEN, Patrick WOLFE, Werner ZIPS and Alan BARNARD
2006 'Discussion: The concept of indigeneity.' *Social Anthropology* 14(1): 17-32.
HADIPRAYITNO, Irene Istiningsih
2010 'Defensive Enforcement: Human Rights in Indonesia.' *Human Rights Review* online (SpringerLink Date 6.10.2009). http://www.springerlink.com/content/d365440027111644/ (accessed 27.4.2010).
HENLEY, David and Jamie S. DAVIDSON
2007 'Introduction: Radical conservatism - the protean politics of adat.' Pp. 1-49 in Davidson and Henley (eds.).
HOROWITZ, Shale and Albrecht SCHNABEL
2004 'Human rights and societies in transition: International context and sources of variation.' Pp. 3-25 in Shale Horowitz and Albrecht Schnabel (eds.), *Human rights and societies in transition: Causes, consequences, responses*. New York: United Nations University Press.
HOWARD, Rhoda E.
1992 'Dignity, Community, and Human Rights'. Pp. 81-102 in Abdullahi Ahmed An-Na'im (ed.), *Human Rights in Cross-Cultural Perspectives: A Quest for Consensus*. Philadelphia: University of Pennsylvania Press.
HUMAN RIGHTS WATCH
1999 *Report on Violence in Ambon*. A Human Rights Watch Report. Vol. 11, No. 1(C), March 1999.
INTERNATIONAL CRISIS GROUP
2000 'Indonesia: Overcoming Murder and Chaos in Maluku.' Asia Report No. 10, 19.12.2000. Jakarta/Brussels.

2002 'Indonesia: The Search for Peace in Maluku.' Asia Report No. 31, 08.02.2002. Jakarta/Brussels.

JACOBSEN, Michael

2002a 'Indonesian Conflicts, A Regional Perspective.' Pp. 31-48 in Kivimäki et al. (eds.).

2002b '"To be or what to be - that is the question": Decentralization and Identity in North Sulawesi.' Pp. 225-255 in Kivimäki et al. (eds.).

JACOBSEN, Michael and Ole BRUUN (eds.)

2000 *Human Rights and Asian Values: Contesting National Identities and Cultural Representations in Asia*. Surrey: Curzon.

JUWANA, Hikmahanto

2006 'Human Rights in Indonesia.' Pp. 364-383 in Randall Peerenboom, Carole J. Petersen and Albert H. Y. Chen (eds.), *Human Rights in Asia: A comparative legal study of twelve Asian jurisdictions, France and the USA*. London/New York: Routledge.

KATO, Tsuyoshi

1989 'Different Fields, Similar Locusts: Adat Communities and the Village Law of 1979 in Indonesia.' *Indonesia* 47 (April): 89-114.

KIVIMÄKI, Timo, Michael JACOBSEN and Pius Suratman KARTASASMITA (eds.)

2002 *Democracy, Decentralization, Identity and Conflict in Indonesia*. Helsinki/Copenhagen: CTS-Conflict Transformation Service.

KLINKEN, Gerry van

2001a 'Indonesia's New Ethnic Elite.' *Workshop 'Indonesia in Transition'* August 2001. http://www.knaw.nl/indonesia/transition/workshop/chapter4vanklinken.pdf (accessed 7.9.2004).

2001b 'The Maluku Wars: Bringing Society Back In.' *Indonesia* 71 (April): 1-26.

2007a *Communal Violence and Democratization in Indonesia: Small town wars*. Routledge Contemporary Southeast Asa Series 15. London/New York: Routledge.

2007b 'Return of the sultans: The communitarian turn in local politics.' Pp. 149-169 in Davidson and Henley (eds.).

KNAAP, G. J.

1987 'Kruidnagelen en Christenen. De Verenigde Oost-Indische Compagnie en de Bevolking van Ambon 1656-1696.' *Verhandelingen van het Koninklijk Instituut voor Taal-, Land- en Volkenkunde* 125. Leiden: KITLV Press.

KREUZER, Peter

2002 *Applying theories of ethno-cultural conflict and conflict resolution to collective violence in Indonesia*. PRIF Report No. 63, Frankfurt am Main.

Peace Research Institute Frankfurt (Hessische Stiftung Friedens- und Konfliktforschung). http://www.hsfk.de/downloads/prifrep63.pdf (accessed 8.11.2004).

KUPER, Adam
2003 'The Return of the Native.' *Current Anthropology* 44(3): 389-402.

LEE, Juliet Patricia
1999 'Out of Order: The Politics of Modernity in Indonesia.' PhD Dissertation (UMI Dissertation Services), University of Virginia.

LEIRISSA, R. Z., John A. PATTIKAYHATU and Soenjata KARTADARMADJA
1982/1983 *Sejarah Sosial di Daerah Maluku*. Ambon: Direktorat Sejarah dan Nilai Tradisional.

LI, Tania M.
2007 'Adat in Central Sulawesi: Contemporary deployments.' Pp. 337-370 in Davidson and Henley (eds.).

LOUNELA, Anu
2004 'Decentralization in Indonesia: Legal changes and emerging forest movements in Central Java.' Paper presented at the 4th EUROSEAS Conference, Paris, 1-4 September 2004.

McCARTHY, John F.
2004 'Changing to Gray: Decentralization and the Emergence of Volatile Socio-legal Configurations in Central Kalimantan, Indonesia.' Asia Research Centre, Murdoch University, Australia January 2004. http://wwwarc.murdoch.edu.au/wp/wp101.pdf (accessed 11.11.2004).

MERRY, Sally Engle
2001 Changing rights, changing culture. Pp. 31-55 in Jane K. Cowan, Marie-Bénédicte Dembour and Richard A. Wilson (eds.), *Culture and Rights: Anthropological Perspectives*. Cambridge: Cambridge University Press.
2005 'Transnational Human Rights and Local Activism: Mapping the Middle.' http://cronus.uwindsor.ca/users/b/basok/main.nsf/6d8ffcfd02afe81e8525730600490ed8/178b2c68bafb979d852576a300533f46/$FILE/ATT128LB/Merry%20AA%202006.pdf (accessed 12.12.2010).
2006 *Human Rights & Gender Violence: Translating International Law into Local Justice*. Chicago/London: The University of Chicago Press.

MESSER, Ellen
1993 'Anthropology and Human Rights.' *Annual Review of Anthropology* 22: 221-249.

OTTO, Ton and Poul PEDERSEN
2005 'Disentangling Traditions: Culture, Agency and Power.' Pp. 11-49 in Ton Otto and Poul Pedersen (eds.), *Tradition and Agency: Tracing Cultural Continuity and Invention*. Aarhus: Aarhus University Press.

PALMER, Blair

2004 'Memories of Migration: Butonese Migrants returning to Buton after the Maluku conflicts 1999–2002.' *Antropologi Indonesia* Special Volume: 87-99. http://www.jai.or.id/jurnal/2004/sv/08bp sv04.pdf (accessed 28.1.2006).

PANNELL, Sandra

2003 'Violence, Society and the State in Eastern Indonesia: Context.' Pp. 11-36 in Pannell (ed.).

PANNELL, Sandra (ed.)

2003 *A State of Emergency: Violence, Society and the State in Eastern Indonesia*. Darwin: Northern Territory University Press.

PARIELA, Tonny D.

1996 'Social Transformation in Soya Atas Village.' Pp. 106-120 in David Mearns and Chris Healey (eds.), *Remaking Maluku. Social Transformation in Eastern Indonesia*. Northern Territory University: Darwin, Australia.

PERMANA, Nurhayat Arif

2002 'Revitalisasi Lembaga Adat dalam Menyelesaikan Konflik Etnis Menghadapi Otonomi Daerah: Studi Kasus Pulau Bangka.' *Antropologi Indonesia* 68: 74-85.

RESOSUDARMO, Ida Aju Pradnja

2003 'Shifting Power to the Periphery: The Impact of Decentralisation on Forests and Forest People.' Pp. 230-244 in Aspinall and Fealy (eds.).

SCHULTE NORDHOLT, Henk

2003 'Renegotiating boundaries: Access, agency and identity in post-Soeharto Indonesia.' *Bijdragen tot de Taal-, Land- en Volkenkunde* 159(4): 550-589.

SCHULTE NORDHOLT, Henk and Gerry van KLINKEN (eds.)

2007 *Renegotiating Boundaries: Local politics in post-Suharto Indonesia*. Leiden: KITLV Press.

SCHULZE, Kirsten E.

2002 'Laskar Jihad and the Conflict in Ambon.' *The Brown Journal of World Affairs* IX(1): 57-69.

SIEDER, Rachel and Jessica WITCHELL

2001 'Advancing indigenous claims through the law: reflections on the Guatemalan peace process.' Pp. 201-225 in Jane K. Cowan, Marie-Bénédicte Dembour and Richard A. Wilson (eds.), *Culture and Rights: Anthropological Perspectives*. Cambridge: Cambridge University Press.

SPYER, Patricia

2002 'Fire without Smoke and other Phantoms of Ambon's Violence: Media

Effects, Agency, and the Work of Imagination.' *Indonesia* 74 (October 2002): 21-36.

THORBURN, Craig C.

2003 'The Plot Thickens: Decentralisation and Land Administration in Indonesia.' Paper presented at the conference *Politics of the Commons: Articulating Development and Strengthening Local Practices*, Chiang Mai, Thailand, July 11-14, 2003. http://dlc.dlib.indiana.edu/archive/00001161/00/Thorburn.pdf (accessed 20.12.2004).

U.S. DEPARTMENT OF STATE

2006 *Indonesia: Country Reports on Human Rights Practices - 2006*. Bureau of Democracy, Human Rights, and Labor.

VINCENT, Joan

2002 'Law.' Pp. 330-333 in Alan Barnard and Jonathan Spencer (eds.), *Encyclopedia of Social and Cultural Anthropology*. London/New York: Routledge.

WIDLOK, Thomas

2007 'Die Last des Erbes: Apartheid, indigenes Recht und Erbrechtsreform in Namibia.' *Zeitschrift für Ethnologie,* Special issue, Birgit Bräuchler and Thomas Widlok (eds.), *Die Revitalisierung von Tradition / The Revitalisation of Tradition* 132: 77-90.

WILSON, Richard Ashby

2006 'Afterword to "Anthropology and Human Rights in a New Key": The Social Life of Human Rights.' *American Anthropologist* 108(1): 77-83.

LEGAL PLURALISM AND MODERNIZATION: AMERICAN LAW PROFESSORS IN ETHIOPIA AND THE DOWNFALL OF THE RESTATEMENTS OF AFRICAN CUSTOMARY LAW

Kaius Tuori

Introduction

In his otherwise insightful contribution, Peter H. Sand presents the history of foreign involvement in the Ethiopian law reform that began in the 1950s as simply a process of modernization and Westernization (Sand 2009).[1] The comprehensive legislative reform in the form of law codes and the establishment of a law school is portrayed as a success story of the 'law and development' movement. There is more to it than that. While Sand maintains that the aim of Western involvement in Ethiopia was the modernization of law in line with the age-old tradition of imposition of foreign law in Africa (Sand 2009: 754)[2], other ideas were presented and experimented with.

[1] While Sand's article is nominally a book review, it addresses a much larger issue on the history Western involvement in the development of Ethiopian law.

[2] As attested by the recollections of his colleague from the Addis Ababa Faculty of Law, Professor Norman J. Singer, in Singer 2008: 137-145.

The purpose of this paper is to explore the involvement of American law professors such as A. Arthur Schiller in a little-known attempt to formulate restatements of indigenous Ethiopian customary law during the 1960s and 1970s to counteract the law reforms. While elsewhere in Africa efforts to improve the administration of law had involved drafting restatements of indigenous customary law, Ethiopia had opted for a wholesale modernization of its legal system through the introduction of codes. Because of claims that this modernization had led to the nullification of law outside the capital, Schiller's project attempted to demonstrate the viability of traditionalism through the revival of indigenous customary law. The article will first discuss the history of the restatement of customary law projects in Africa, before moving to Schiller and the situation in Ethiopia and finally to the wider discussion on law reform, pluralism, and modernization. In the process, the article will discuss changes in the concept of normative pluralism (Twining 2010) and its relationship to colonialism and the law and development movement.

There were two models of legal reform, namely, modernization and traditionalism, offered to Africa by the American law professors and their European colleagues involved in the reforms. Modernization or traditionalism as tools for reform were alternative modes of action embedded in Western legal traditions, with predecessors from the German nineteenth century struggle for law reform to the American 'restatement of law' movement. The aim of this article is to question the assumption of a single line of legal development in Africa and show variations by comparisons in which developments in Ethiopia are juxtaposed with developments in former British Africa, and the restatement project of Schiller is compared with the far larger British programs.

The story of Schiller and his project is important for the history of legal pluralism because it shows how modernization of law, legal education, and restatements of law coexisted with legal pluralism and the legacy of colonialism in Africa. The preservation of indigenous law was widely seen as a viable alternative to modernization and Westernizing legal reforms. Even though the project was not successful, and partly just because it was not, it reveals the complexity of intellectual developments, which are too often shown teleologically through the wisdom of hindsight.[3]

---

[3] Numerous conferences on the matter were organized and their proceedings published: Rijksuniversiteit Te Leiden 1956. Schiller 1960, in a note in the 'Notes and News' section of the *Journal of African Law* mentions a colloquium in Brussels discussing the activities of Jacques Vanderlinden in the Belgian areas, J.

As an alternative to the imposition of Western law, African nationalists argued that modernizing legal reforms in Africa should be complemented by the study of indigenous legal traditions such as customary law (Nkrumah 1962: 104). The plural legal systems in Africa were a product of the colonial period and operated either by recognizing the jurisdiction of traditional conflict resolution mechanisms or through courts which handled cases involving indigenous peoples. In order to make such a system more acceptable to judiciaries accustomed to written laws and proceedings, collections and restatements of indigenous law were made around the continent.[4]

The study relies on two sets of archival sources, the A. Arthur Schiller Papers at the Columbia University Rare Book and Manuscript Library[5] and the collection of papers of the Restatement of African Law Project in the archives of the School of Oriental and African Studies in London.[6]

A. Arthur Schiller, African Customary Law, and Modernization

The wholesale modernization of the legal system undertaken by Ethiopia was an anomaly in the African context. The incorporation of indigenous law in the legal system was a concern all over Africa during the interwar years and continuing to the 1960s (Lewin 1938; Allott 1957; Haydon 1960: vii-xi.), but after independence African countries were often torn between the contradictory impulses of preserving the traditional African legal heritage and the demands of modernization, progress, and nation building.[7]

Poirier in the French areas, and A. N. Allott for the British and former British territories, while discussing also the American, Indian, Islamic and Indonesian restatements of law. Schiller 1960: 65.

[4] For critical views of the process, see: Roberts and Mann 1991; Moore 1992; Chanock 1985, 2001. It should be noted that informal courts existed and continue to exist independently of state structures: see Burman and Schärf 1990.

[5] A. Arthur Schiller Papers 1897-1977, MS#1125 Rare Book & Manuscript Library, Columbia University in the City of New York.

[6] School of Oriental and African Studies: Restatement of African Law Project, reference code GB 0102 PP MS 74.

[7] See, for example Nkrumah 1962; Woodman and Obilade 1995; Kuper and Kuper

The majority of states in Africa went through similar developments in their legal systems in which the law introduced by the Europeans was often adapted and retained even after independence.[8] During the period under consideration, from the 1950s to the 1970s, two parallel developments took place throughout Africa bringing the indigenous native culture and the Westernized legal systems closer: first, restatements of indigenous law were made by legal scholars, and second, law schools were founded to educate the local population about the legal system.[9]

From the late 1950s, a group of mainly British scholars including Antony Allott and his team from the School of Oriental and African Studies in London compiled restatements of African customary law for the soon to be former British Africa. Allott's Restatement of African Law project (RALP, 1959-1977) was by far the largest and most systematic effort to collect the rules of traditional native law in writing. The outline of the project called for a standardized and scientific approach to restatements, with a bibliographical stage, the assembly of the material and the actual recording by field workers, for which a five-year period was reserved. The field workers took part in the meetings of law panels and attempted to reconstruct the social and legal framework.[10] The aim of the project was to "record the law as currently applied", even if it varied from tradition.[11]

1965. The role that customary law played after independence varied, often according to the level of integration and complicity of the native courts in the colonial system. In Zimbabwe, where the state structures had incorporated the customary law courts, they were to a large extent replaced, but in places like Mozambique, Malawi and Tanzania legal pluralism continued despite some attempts at instituting a national legal system: Chanock 1991: 60. On West Africa, see Woodman 1969.

[8] Schiller 1966: 997. See Asante 1987 for an analysis of the issues encountered by Ghana in dealing with materials from British, customary and indigenous law.

[9] There were also attempts at formulating an indigenous African legal theory: see Elias 1956.

[10] Cotran 1987; Read 1987; Moore 1992: 23; The School of Oriental and African Studies (SOAS): Restatement of African Law Project Papers (RALP), PP MS 74, box 26a: Proceedings of the meeting of 3.10.61 to discuss future activities of the project; box 30: Bulambia, Misuku Law Panel meetings December 1-3, 1963 with J. O. Ibik, Customary Law Commissioner, SOAS, as chairman.

[11] SOAS: RALP, PP MS 74, box 26a: Minutes of RALP, March 2, 1965.

From 1969 onwards several collections of restatements were published by RALP from Kenya (Cotran 1968, 1969), Malawi (Ibik 1970, 1971), Botswana (Roberts 1972), and Ghana (Kludze 1973), and work continued until 1977 concerning most of the British colonies and former colonies in Africa. Looking at the project's correspondence and research plans it is possible to follow the intellectual interest first rising in the 1960s and later turning against the project. The period of 1960 to 1970 was marked by the growth of the organization and its plans and optimism,[12] while the 1970s was a time of gradual withdrawal and abandonment. From the early '70s it is evident that many of the local partners began to lose interest in the restatements. Though the preparation of existing book projects and the planning of new ones continued, with at one point eleven writers working on separate projects, negative signals were appearing. For example, F. M. Ssekandi, the director of the Law Development Centre in Kampala, was planning to start a restatement of law project along the lines of the RALP restatements in 1972 and sought assistance, but the official government position was against any such project and nothing came of it. The RALP even began to organize events on the codification of laws in Africa.[13]

Columbia law professor A. Arthur Schiller (1902-1977) began a similar restatement of customary law project that focused on Ethiopia and Eritrea in co-operation with the law school in Addis Ababa. He was one of the undisputed pioneers of legal pluralism. A specialist in Roman law, Indonesian law, African law, and military law, he was a polyglot and interdisciplinary talent, rare traits for American law professors at the time. His early interest in indigenous customary law from the 1930s to the 1950s gave him a unique position when the study of African law became increasingly relevant in the early 1960s. Schiller founded the African Law Center at Columbia in 1965, which was the first institute of African Law in the US. *African Law Studies*, the center's journal, is now the *Journal of Legal Pluralism and Unofficial Law*. At Columbia Law School was also John Bainbridge, who directed the SAILER (Project on Staffing of African Institutions of Legal Education and Research, 1962-1972, included in 1965 in the International

[12] SOAS: RALP, PP MS 74, box 26a: Minutes of RALP, November 7, 1962.

[13] SOAS: RALP, PP MS 74, box 26a, F. M. Ssekandi to A. N. Allott, letters 3rd and 30th August 1972, box 26b, A. N. Allott, memo on the projected conference on the Codification and Unification of Laws in Africa, June 19, 1973 and Proceedings of the Study Group on Unification and Codification of Laws in Africa.

Legal Center) project from 1962 to 1972.[14]

In 1951 Schiller became a United Nations legal consultant for Eritrea, drawing up a draft constitution for the state.[15] That brief involvement led Schiller to take a wider interest in the development of African law and he began to teach African law at Columbia, according to himself the first to do so in a U.S. law school. In his teaching he presented his vision of legal pluralism as the future of African law in which law would be pluralistic, with at least two systems, indigenous and non-indigenous coexisting.[16]

Schiller's main African research project was the collection and translation of the customary laws of land tenure in Tigray, which he referred to as: "a project devoted to a survey of restatements of customary law on the part of the indigenous population." The Tigray area in Northern Ethiopia and Eritrea already had numerous restatements of customary law in existence. These restatements, called *fethas*, the earliest of which were from the nineteenth century, recorded the customary law of the plateau people, written in the Tigrinya language. The purpose of the project was to:

> [C]all to the attention of Ethiopian judges a vital element of indigenous law, now wholly discounted. The last few years have shown that the enactment and attempted application of a Civil Code based on principles of western law (continental European and Anglo-American) has led to severe nullification of the law outside the bounds of Addis Ababa and a few other cities. The

---

[14] A. Arthur Schiller folder, Historical Biographical Files Collection, Box 282, Folder 3, University Archives, Rare Book & Manuscript Library, Columbia University in the City of New York; NY Times, July 12, 1977.

[15] A. Arthur Schiller Papers 1897-1977, MS#1125 Rare Book & Manuscript Library, Columbia University in the City of New York (Schiller papers), box 29, Eritrea - Correspondence and speeches, Letter of appointment, Consultant in the Secretariat of the United Nations, Asmara, Eritrea, July 6, 1951- Oct 5, 1951; Schiller papers, box 29, Eritrean II, 17 Aug 1951, To: His Excellency the United Nations Commissioner, Summary Report on Possible Conflict of Jurisdictions, Sep 7, 1951, Draft Constitution for Eritrea.

[16] Schiller papers, box 31, African Law, file Seminar in African Law, proposal for a seminar in African law to be held 1959-1960.

> existence of a large mass of indigenous legal doctrine, capable of being modified to satisfy ever-changing needs, should do much to restore faith and respect for a deep cultural heritage, and at the same time provide a basis for sensible modernization of the law.[17]

The choice of Ethiopia was particularly apt. In its drive to modernization, Ethiopia had pursued a far-reaching legal reform program in a series of codifications. The Penal Code of 1957 was followed by the Civil Code of 1960 drafted with the help of the famous French expert in comparative law, René David. David described the ideas behind the reform of civil law:

> While safeguarding certain traditional values to which she remains profoundly attached, Ethiopia wishes to modify her structures completely, even to the way of life of her people. Consequently Ethiopians do not expect the new Code to be a work of consolidation ... of actual customary rules. They wish it to be a program envisaging a total transformation of society and they demand that for the most part, it set out new rules appropriate for the society they wish to create. (David 1963: 193)

The Civil Code was in turn followed by the Commercial and Maritime Code of 1961 and the Civil Procedure Code of 1967. Among legal comparativists, the Ethiopian Civil Law codification stood as an example of the dangers of legislative hubris. Regardless of its merits as a codification, it was not applied in practice outside the cities (Brietzke 1975: 48). What attracted Schiller was that there were a number of areas in which the civil code left room for the application of customary law, one of them being the laws of land tenure in the northern provinces of Ethiopia.[18]

An essential part of the legal reforms was the foundation of a law school and a law journal. The tone of reform and progress was apparent in the Inaugural Statement of the Emperor Haile Selassie I in the first issue of the Journal of Ethiopian Law in

[17] Schiller papers, box 29, African Law, file Fetha project, Summary Report to Dean Cordier on Summer 1966 travel and research by A. Arthur Schiller.

[18] Schiller 1969: 2-3. Schiller noted that actually René David made a careful study of the Ethiopian customary laws and attempted to incorporate them into the code, but these adaptations were stricken from the code by the Ethiopian codification commission.

1964. The modernization of the legal system and Ethiopia's rapid progress demanded the services of a large number of legal experts, the emperor wrote:

> Law is a unifying force in a nation: one of the goals sought to be attained by the enactment of modern codes and other legislation is that the law be uniform throughout the Empire. (Haile Sellassie I 1964: v)

The journal was meant to be the vehicle for the development and dissemination of an Ethiopian interpretation of the codes, just as the Addis Ababa University[19] law school, founded in 1963, was meant to produce legal experts to serve as judges, advocates, administrators and police. The law school had by 1967 close to 700 students in its various programs in English and Amharic. Funding for the school came mostly from the Ford Foundation, and the professors were for the most part international, with Americans being the largest group. During the early years, the deans were all American, James C. N. Paul being the founding dean, followed by Quintin Johnstone and Cliff F. Thompson (Paul 1967).

The founding of the law school in Addis Ababa was part of a wider trend and the growing interest in law in Africa. From the early 1960s onwards, faculties of law were founded in African countries with the help of Western scholars and institutions. Projects like the SAILER program were used to bring Western law professors to teach for a few years in African universities while giving opportunities and scholarships to African teachers and students to study in North American and European law schools. Ford Foundation funding was crucial to many of the NGO projects, while the US government participated with the Peace Corps and USAID projects often interlinked with NGOs. While the projects had a development agenda of training lawyers and professors, who would then be able to teach the judges, lawyers and administrators that these newly independent countries needed after the colonial administration was removed, during the Cold War there was also political importance in the question, who would train the future ruling elites of Africa. However, one must not underestimate the spirit of optimism of the era and the belief in development.[20]

---

[19] Known at the time as 'Haile Sellassie I University'.

[20] Paul shows how already in 1962 American law professors were active in numerous African countries, with American deans heading law schools in Ghana (W. B. Harvey) and Nigeria (George Johnson) (Paul 1962-1963; see also: Johnstone 1971-1972: 657; Paul 1987: 20-21). A more somber tone is apparent in

The intellectual climate in which any project of legal reform in Africa operated was marked by the contradictory relationship between tradition and progress. To some of the nationalist governments of Africa, the colonial heritage tainted indigenous customary law and the native courts, while there was also a need to reject any alien imposition in their legal system. There was simultaneously a will to validate indigenous law that would reflect African culture and values and to reform institutions in the name of progress and national unity. Traditional authorities such as tribal chiefs and the native courts system had often been the tools of colonial rule, which had supported and controlled them. Many of the independence movements were committed to the idea of development and modernization, and adhering to the tribal administration with its often hereditary traditional leaders and systems of ownership would have been an unnecessary hindrance to development (Bennett 2009; Bennett 2004: 17-18; Allott 1970, 13-14; Peters 2009: 1317–1325).

The Reanimation of a Lost Tradition, Pluralism and Colonialism

Even in Ethiopia, there was considerable interest in indigenous customary law. The professors of the law school, mainly relatively recent law graduates with some having advanced degrees, were active writers for the Ethiopian Law Journal. The majority of articles concerned the interpretation of the Ethiopian law codes, but the fact that customary law had been allowed some room was a matter of controversy among the professors of the law school (for example: Krzectunowicz 1966; Vanderlinden 1966; David 1967). Though there was interest in the content of customary law and the functioning of traditional courts, the foreign law school professors were behind a language barrier that prevented most of them from engaging with the customary legal material.

While the professors of the Addis Ababa law school were products of a modern Western legal training and taught the thoroughly modern official legal system of Ethiopia to their students, Schiller was from a very different background. Schiller's thinking on legal pluralism was a product of his rather unusual interests. In the field of Roman law, he specialized in Coptic legal texts, a small subfield studying mostly Egyptian materials. In comparative and indigenous law, he spent over a decade studying Indonesian indigenous *Adat* law, and after that over two decades involved in African law. All of these three fields included legal pluralism

the ILC volumes on law and development: ILC 1974, 1975.

of different kinds, starting from the situation in Roman Egypt, in which a number of competing legal systems had coexisted.

Schiller's method of inquiry was based on a combination of case law and legal tradition, comparing the decisions of local courts and tribal authorities (Schiller 1962). To Schiller, law was based on the culture of the people and it was the task of legal scholars to reduce it to universal rules. This essentialist view of law was based on nineteenth century German legal theory, which stressed the long connection between law and culture. It took centuries for laws to adapt to a culture and for the people to develop an affinity to them. Making rash changes via legislative reform or codification only served to alienate people from the laws, because one could not legislate tradition (Whitman 1990: 120-234).

As with Indonesia, Schiller's earlier interest, the future of African law would be determined by the policy chosen, there being essentially three options: 1) pluralism, 2) the abolition of the indigenous system and the institution of a Western-oriented one, or 3) "a national legal system" that "may be established by directed evolution of the law, fusing the plural legal systems into one, as in the British, French and Belgian areas." According to Schiller, the means available for this directed legal evolution were legislation, a restatement of indigenous law, judicial decisions by tribunals, native or otherwise, scientific anthropological studies, and a trained legal profession.[21]

While the first option, pluralism, had been the practice of colonial regimes and the second, legal imposition, the ultimate aim of colonialism, which option would the independent nations choose? Ethiopia had made a very strong move towards Westernization, while former colonies might continue as they had in pluralistic systems, to follow Ethiopia in wholesale modernization, or try to fuse the traditions together. On paper, it would appear that in all three options restatements of customary law were needed, even in the Ethiopian style modernization as Schiller had argued.

While the practice of the 'tribes and traditions' style of legal anthropological

[21] Schiller papers, box 31, African Law, file Seminar in African Law, proposal for a seminar in African law to be held 1959-1960: "I call to your attention to the fact that this would be another Columbia first, with other law schools offering a similar seminar, I am certain, within a few years."

scholarship[22] had been to collect a priori sets of rules by interviewing informants such as tribal elders, Schiller opposed the study of customs and rules for their own sake and claimed that it was only with a determination such as a court judgment that one reached law. Schiller thought that the whole concept of customary law was misleading and should be abandoned because law revealed itself only in a judicial determination. Legal custom was turned into law, but it was not customary law, but judge-made law. According to Schiller, only by establishing a trained judiciary could African legal traditions be adapted with legislation to serve the changing circumstances of the present. Even though he did not concur with the claims of Indonesian nationalists, who argued that the system of *Adat* law was simply an artificial collection of ancient customs, he saw the argument as a suitable warning against fostering concepts such as customary law. His belief was that people should build up their own traditions, including law, and that labeling indigenous law archaic and primitive, which had been the meaning of the label 'customary law', was hardly helpful.[23]

As interpretations of native law by Western or Western-educated lawyers, the restatement projects in Africa like those produced by the RALP were intended to be compatible with a Western or a Western-influenced legal system such as those set up by colonial administrations and operating in the cities of African countries. However, Ethiopia was a case of its own, having never been colonized despite the Italian occupation prior to and during the Second World War. Schiller's aim was to circumvent the problem of Western influence by using earlier material that would have been free of such influence. As Schiller well knew, the influence of foreign law in Ethiopia dates back to the seventeenth century and the translation of the canon law code *Fetha Nagast*, or the Law of the Kings, which incorporated material from the Byzantine law books (Sand 2009: 757-758). Whether there were any legal compilations that would not have contained some foreign influence is unclear, but the use of very old materials posed its own problems. The renewal of the old would have required a living tradition of interpretation to adapt to the modern world. As in the case of the attempt to formulate a law reform with the use of ancient Roman material in nineteenth-century Germany, the reanimation was

[22] The classic of the scientific orientation of the rule centered approach was Schapera 1938.

[23] Schiller 1936: 259; Schiller 1966: 997; A. Arthur Schiller, 'Custom and Customary Law – Primitive Societies', Lecture at Aberdeen, May 1957, Schiller papers, box 31, African Law, file Correspondence and African Law Material, pages 7, 11, 13.

not successful because there was no living tradition and no effort to create one. The search for purity produced sterility (Whitman 1990: 221-228).

During his travels in Ethiopia during the late 1960s and early 1970s Schiller gathered a number of *fethas* and other Ethiopian customary law collections. His aim was to publish a compilation of the available restatements with an English translation and commentary, English being the main common language of legal scholars in Ethiopia. He was especially interested in the laws of land tenure, which were of utmost importance in a region marked by strife between nomadic and sedentary peoples. The translation process of the *fethas* revealed another fundamental error in Schiller's project. Because Schiller had sought to uncover the earliest and most authentic texts, they were in fact quite impossible for a modern Tigrinyan speaker to understand. Thus instead of recording a living tradition, Schiller was actually translating ancient texts. Locals undoubtedly referred to these as the source of law, but, as often happens in legal reasoning, the interpretation had long since left the original intent behind. Although the translations were made, the eventual publication of the *fethas* progressed very slowly and the deteriorating political situation in Ethiopia did little to help matters.[24]

The extent of the institution building done by Schiller underlines how much he was also committed to the ideas of modernization and reform. Schiller's African Law Center at Columbia University, funded by Ford Foundation grants, handled the practical administration of the various Africa projects. The main task of the center was the publication of the *African Law Digest*, which followed legislation and case law in Africa, and the academic journal *African Law Studies*. At Columbia, the daily operation of the African Law Center was entrusted to a series of assistant directors, among them John Bruce, Cliff Thompson, and Jeswald Salacuse.[25]

By 1970, time was working against Schiller because he had begun the project quite

---

[24] Schiller papers, box 36, Ethiopian Law, A-F, Customary Law Project, The Written law of HabSellus, GhebreKristos, DeKeteshum; Schiller papers, box 36, Ethiopian Law, A-F, Ethiopia project (Tesfazim), Schiller to Mr Tesfatsion Medhanie, Law School, Addis Feb 22, 1971; J. T. Harrison to Schiller May 10, 1972, of three compilations, Law of Logo and Chewa, Law of Seharti, and Lamza, Schiller to Jeremy T. Harrison, June 6, 1972. One of the main problems appeared to be the lack of translators from Tigrinya to English.

[25] Apparently the administration was relatively informal as some of the assistant directors had no recollection of the fact that they were assistant directors.

late in his career. Even the institutional background was fading. As Schiller retired from Columbia in 1971, the direction of the African Law Center was given to Robert Hellawell. It was also decided that the center would be moved to Addis Ababa, along with its publications, as parts of the law school. After his retirement, Schiller continued to work on the *fetha* project, but began to concentrate his energy on writing a book on Roman law.[26]

While Schiller was recognized by his contemporaries as a pioneer in the field of African law,[27] his work was too tied to current legal affairs to endure and Schiller has been largely forgotten. The publication of the customary law project was never completed, partly due to the fact that the 1974-1975 socialist revolution in Ethiopia removed both the need and the possibilities for research.[28] By the late 1970s the general enthusiasm of the law and development movement was evaporating and critical voices were appearing, for example accusing it of doing missionary work for legal liberalism.[29]

While Schiller's project and the RALP had similar chronologies and phases of development, although the RALP began earlier and ended later, there were fundamental differences. In contrast to Schiller's work in independent Ethiopia, the RALP had both the advantage and the disadvantage of building on the foundation of the British colonial practice in the application of indigenous law. The indirect rule of the British was founded on certain basic principles, such as the judicial ascertainment of customary law and the personality principle. The judicial ascertainment was twofold, the courts would first ascertain the content of the native custom and then find out whether it could apply it. The rules were discovered from tribal practice, from evidence given by the tribal chiefs and

[26] Schiller papers, box 23, Learned Societies C-I, file International African Law Association, Encyclopaedia of African Law, letter to Jacques Vanderlinden July 19, 1975. The book on Roman law, Schiller 1978, appeared posthumously.

[27] Schiller papers, box 26 African Law Abel-African Law Material (1), file African Law, ALAA Correspondence, June 21, 1971, letter from David N. Smith to Schiller: "I am sorry that African legal studies is losing you. We Africanists are all indebted to you for your pioneering work."

[28] A similar project was completed recently through a collaboration of an Italian and an American legal scholar: Favali and Pateman 2003.

[29] See Paul 1987: 26 for references.

elders, and from case law.[30] In application, the rule was that courts should be guided by native law as far as the law was not repugnant to natural justice or morality or to any legislation, to use, for example, the 1898 decree in Southern Rhodesia (current Zimbabwe).[31] The personality principle meant in the context of indirect rule that cases between natives were settled using indigenous law while cases between Europeans were subject to Western law. In matters like family law Islamic law was also applied.[32]

Even between various British colonies, the approach taken by colonial administrators to customary law varied. In places like Kenya, where the native courts were under the administration, not the judiciary, it was a deeply held conviction that the best option would be to allow the law to remain flexible and

---

[30] Allott 1970: 258; Shadle 1999. See Lewin for a contemporary view on the various issues encountered by the British on the ascertainment of the content of indigenous law (Lewin 1938: 18-20). The case law for the use of customary law in British Africa was mainly from Southern and Western Africa. Application of Native Law permissible: *Cole v Cole*, 1898, *Nigerian Law Reports I*: 21; *Komo and Leboho v Holmes*, N.O., 1935, S. Rhodesia, 86; *Nqanoyi's case*, 1930, Native Appeal Court (Cape), vol. ii, p. 18. Contra, see *Vela v Mandinika and Magutsa*, 1936, S. Rhodesia, 171. The use of chiefs as sources of law: *Hermansberg Mission Society v Commissioner for Native Affairs and Darius Mogalie*, 1906, Transvaal Supreme Court, p. 135; *Lewis v Bankole*, 1909, *Nigerian Law Reports I*: 82; *Visram v Gwanombi*, East African Law Reports, vol. vi (1915-1916), p. 31. Custom as existing from time immemorial: *Angu v Attah* (1916) Gold Coast Privy Council Judgments (1874-1928), p. 43.

[31] This *repugnancy test* was in different forms applied in all British colonies in Africa.It was confirmed by case law and legislation: Nigeria and the Gold Coast Supreme Court Ordinance, 1876, s. 19; Transvaal Law No 4 of 1885; Southern Rhodesia Order in Council, 1898, s. 50; Kenya Order in Council, 1921, s. 7; South African Native Administration Act, No 38, 1927, s. 11.

[32] Sand 2009: 756-757; Lewin 1947; Salacuse 1975; Anderson 1954. For example in Southern Rhodesia the Native Law and Courts Act (1937) ruled that between natives the decision of the court shall be "in accordance with native law and custom". This task was given to the native courts, while it was also recognized that unofficial courts would exist. A native was by definition "any person who is a native of South Africa or of Central Africa." See Goldin and Gelfand 1975: 8-10, 21.

fluid in order for it to be able to adapt to changing circumstances. In places where native courts were placed under the judiciary, there was a more concerted effort to reduce the rules of customary law to writing (Chanock 1985: 51; Shadle 1999).

According to Allott, the British had a number of reasons for supporting indigenous customary laws, ranging from a willingness to maintain tranquility to economy. In line with the idea of indirect rule, relatively few colonial officers were in charge of administering large areas and thus the administration of justice would have been too much of a burden. In many cases the British had explicitly agreed to recognize indigenous law when assuming jurisdiction. It was also claimed that British law would have been too sophisticated for the primitive native populations.[33]

One of the motivations behind the RALP was concern for the future of customary law at the end of colonial indirect rule. With the 'protective barrier' of indirect rule and its separate systems of courts and administration gone, what would become of customary law (Read 1987: 5)? The new nations would need to develop state structures rapidly and with them, to reform their legal systems. By 1960 there were long standing efforts to make collections of rules or restatements of tribal law at least in the French and Belgian African colonies. While those projects, similar to the RALP, were commonly parts of the colonial administration or ethnographic studies, the RALP was conceived as a postcolonial program for the advancement of the administration of law.[34]

The project of Schiller and the RALP also faced similar theoretical obstacles. At a seminar organized at the Haile Sellassie I University in January 1966, Allott and others noted that a restatement project normally encountered problems not only in finding but also in describing customary law. The first solution, as applied in the Natal Native Code of 1896, was to use the existing technical vocabulary of Western law. The ethnocentrism of this approach led Dutch scholars of Indonesian *Adat* law to adopt a neutral descriptive tone, while comparative lawyers tried to create a universal legal language, and anthropologists maintained that one should use indigenous terms in order not to destroy their meaning (Allott, Epstein and Gluckman 1969: 16). In the RALP restatements and other restatement projects the audience was always the judiciary and administration, who both worked in English. Though scholars were acutely aware of the conceptual problems that

[33] Allott 1970: 9-14; Schiller papers, box 31, file Jes Salacuse, Salacuse to Schiller, Nov 26, 1967.

[34] Schiller 1960: 65. Of the Belgian colonies, see Reyntjens 1992.

plagued the colonial usage of indigenous law, a satisfactory solution eluded them.

The Downfall and Survival of African Customary Law through Modernization and Legal Pluralism

In the eyes of modern observers, the colonial model of legal pluralism contained two fundamental errors that led to the downfall of many of the restatement projects: first, that the material they drew on was mainly the interpretation of Western-educated lawyers on indigenous law that would then be applied in practice by Western-style law courts and second, that it gave legal validity and permanence to the views of old tribal leaders and stifled progress. It was apparent in the beginning of the 1970s that the resurrection of traditional customary law systems was not high on the agenda for nationalist African leaders.[35]

However, pluralistic legal systems continue to exist on a large scale, for example in South Africa legal pluralism in its various forms, from the British and Apartheid era state legal pluralism to the current deep legal pluralism, has been the rule for two centuries and there are detailed studies of the practice. As van Niekerk has pointed out, there is a distinct separation between state-law pluralism and deep legal pluralism. In state-law pluralism, the state recognizes customary or other legal rules of certain groups if they fulfill certain tests regulated by the state such as the repugnancy clause, while deep legal pluralism is based on the claim that the state legal system is irrelevant for the existence of unofficial laws (van Niekerk 2001, 2006: 5-10; Chanock 1996).

Lauren Benton has argued that in colonial situations the drafters of the system of indirect rule formulated their own version of legal pluralism in which indigenous systems of law were misrepresented and served as hierarchically lower appendages to state authority. This form of pluralism installed the colonial overlords as the ultimate authority with power to decide what is right and just (Benton 2002: 164-165). The state legal pluralism they practiced was, in effect, merely a category in a very universalistic system that had a clear hierarchy.

Martin Chanock has argued that the version of legal pluralism which was left and remained in Africa as a legacy of colonialism is a kind of dualism, or binary

[35] Bennett 2004: 17-18. See Brietzke (1975) for a contemporary view of law as an obstacle to development.

system, in which the main part of the population is in a subordinate position under a legal system that guarantees them inferior legal rights. Colonial and post-colonial legal systems in Africa have been marked by an extreme legal formalism untempered by the influence of civil society (Chanock 2001: 32). The contrast between the rigid formalism of the state legal system and the informality of customary law made the meeting of the two problematic. The colonial system of indirect rule depended on the conception of well-defined groups which were defined by their immutable legal customs. What the colonial officers and the makers of the restatements after them attempted to do was to put this custom in writing by selecting the cases and rules which would best describe the essence of the custom. The result was that what had once been a living tradition of solving conflicts was now petrified into a set of rules which in themselves were the product of selection and competing claims.[36]

Schiller's view of legal pluralism could best be described as one inspired by comparative law scholarship. In legal pluralism the task of the jurist was to ensure that the indigenous law could be presented in such a form that it could be applied by the courts. Even though it would appear that Schiller advocated state legal pluralism, matters are not that simple. The idea was that indigenous law existed independently of state structures. Schiller brought legal pluralism developed in the Dutch *Adat* school to replace the concept of customary law with pluralism to erase the assumption of the subjection of native law to state law. In such a system, not only legal scholars but also state courts should have the expertise to apply indigenous law.

Like many of his contemporaries, Schiller overlooked the adverse effects of Western colonialism on indigenous law and did not question the authenticity of the indigenous law that was applied by the state legal system. As Shadle has argued, the aim of most of the projects in putting native law in writing was to make them reproducible. Thus they would provide guidance for the administration and satisfy the need for certainty in the law. Even in the 1940s, the British Colonial Office recognized the dangers of codifying customary law, namely, that it would fundamentally alter the fluid operation of changing tradition to adapt to altering conditions by crystallizing customs to a rigid set of rules (Shadle 1999: 411-413; Read 1987: 10).

[36] Chanock 1985: 9. See Asante 1987: 86-87, for the practical problems posed by the demands of judicial notice.

Even during the colonial period it was recognized that observers such as lawyers or anthropologists studying customary law had a tendency to force the logic of Western law on to native law and thus to discover customary law comparable with the legal system known to the researcher. Simply defining customary law in terms of a European system of law led to inaccuracies because of the considerable baggage legal concepts brought along from one legal system to another. A further development removing the indigenous population from their supposed laws was that instead of relying on often contradictory native informants, colonial courts tended to prefer judicial practice as precedent and were allowed to make law when precedent was not found. Furthermore, in urbanized and industrialized areas like regions of South Africa there was the issue of detribalization, or whether one should apply customary law to urbanized people who lived outside any tribal areas and not under any customary authority. The issue of detribalization was accentuated by the fact that tribes as administrative entities were often constructed artificially by colonial administrators, a policy taken furthest in South Africa.[37]

Allott's response in 1987 to these criticisms, that customary law was either a colonial relic and hindrance to development or that the very act of recording would radically alter it by petrification was an argument for realism. First, that legal development should be internal, and that alien impositions, as shown by so many examples, are doomed to fail. Second, that customary law was an existing fact within African legal systems and to be effectively and justly administered there had to be full analytical understanding of them (Allott 1987: 17).

Though he supported the same arguments of tradition and rule of law, Schiller's pluralism followed the model of the Indonesian *Adat* law in which several independent and indigenous systems of law coexisted.[38] Furthermore, Schiller's work on legal pluralism cannot be separated from his studies on Roman law. Schiller did not study Roman law as it is traditionally studied, as the foundation of the civilian tradition of law and a collection of legal rules and institutions. Rather, he studied Roman law as it was applied in practice, drawing from the ideas of

[37] Goldin and Gelfand 1975; Quinlan 1988; Moore 1992. For a contemporary view, see Bennett 2004. The most extreme form of transformation of customary law was the South African codification contained in the Natal Native Code of 1891.

[38] Hoebel and Schiller 1948: 13. On *Adat* law and van Vollenhoven, see Fasseur 1992. On the later studies on *Adat*, see von Benda-Beckmann and Vermeulen 2001.

legal realism which surrounded him at Columbia law school. Schiller was a specialist in legal papyrology and Coptic law, a field which studies the culturally complex and legally pluralistic Egypt in the Roman period. [39]

As in Indonesia, the main source of controversy in Africa was not customary law in itself, but rather the struggle between traditionalism and modernization.[40] The main reason why many of the restatement projects in Africa failed was that Western scholars were producing something that was of little interest to the new African leaders. The issue for the new cadre of leaders was modernization and development. What projects like Schiller's collection of ancient laws provided was a turn to the past, a past with unchangeable rules.

Modernization projects such as the law school in Addis Ababa were some of the battlegrounds in which this struggle between traditionalism and modernization was fought. It was also a battleground between different types of modernization, the capitalist and socialist models. As the political struggle in Ethiopia culminated in the ousting of the emperor and the socialist-inspired military takeover by the Derg in 1974-1975, direct action eclipsed reforms. Tragically, many of the law school graduates did not survive the Red Terror of the early Derg period. While many students became radicalized and participated in the movement to oust the emperor and create the new Socialist Ethiopia, others became suspect under the new regime because of their Western education.

In practice legal pluralism continued as the codes remained unused in the countryside. One of the most popular actions of the Derg was the institution of land reform, which nationalized land previously held by the aristocracy and the church. How much this benefited the Tigray region is open to debate, because the region was dominated by resistance movements and warfare during most of the Derg and Socialist periods. At least the need for a restatement of customary rules of land tenure was reduced by the nationalization of land (Kidane 1990).

---

[39] Schiller 1932: 3-5, 18-20; Schiller 1971.

[40] Schiller 1936: 261-263; Schiller 1942: 31. According to Schiller, the opponents of pluralism claimed that "eventually the higher, more moral, European law will prevail over the more primitive eastern law" (Schiller 1942: 37). Independent Indonesia later opted to develop Western style law codes, while *Adat* law still applies in rural areas in the village level (Fasseur 1992: 255-256). The evolution of studies on *Adat* have been considerable (Gluckman 1949; Hooker 1978; Davidson and Henley 2007).

In current debates the very definition of legal pluralism is controversial. Much of the disagreement follows from the different traditions of pluralism, those of anthropology, comparative law, and international law. While small scale anthropological projects tend to follow the postcolonial antagonism towards state law as oppressive to indigenous peoples, the approach of legally oriented scholarship is very different.[41] Closer to what Schiller was proposing is the deep legal pluralism aspired to currently in South Africa. The practically oriented deep legal pluralism project seeks to harmonize the different legal systems such as Roman-Dutch law, common law, customary law, unofficial customary law, Islamic law, Hindu law, Jewish law, and people's law, in addition to the various official and unofficial court systems, to "a legal system which revolves around a core of parallel, yet different residual sources" (van Niekerk 2006: 14).[42] Both the anthropological and comparative law approaches to legal pluralism should be separated from the idea of global legal pluralism, which deals with the rules of international legal norms, human rights, NGOs, and migration (Tamanaha 2008: 20-36, 63)[43].

What the example of Schiller and his project may show is that the best of intentions and the use of advanced methods are of little use when political developments are not favorable. The projects of legal reform were swept away by the revolution, but it is doubtful whether Schiller's endeavor would have been successful even without the revolution. Pluralism does not work artificially, as Schiller well grasped in theory, and, as the South African examples show, no legal tradition will live in writing if it is not part of the social reality. The uniting factor between the colonial systems, the Restatement of African Law Project and Schiller's project was the belief in the neutrality of recording. While the RALP and Schiller strove to free themselves from the tradition of the imposition of law, they could not translate and transfer the law neutrally to writing because of the very impossibility of reducing a living system to a set of rules. That does not mean that the restatements are not used in practice, quite the contrary (Read 1987: 11).

[41] The growth of the conflict between the legal and social anthropological approaches is evident in the debates in Allott and Woodman 1985.

[42] Bennett 2006 points out that the price of legal pluralism is the perpetuation of conflicts of laws (Bennett 2006: 25-27).

[43] On the debate over pluralism, see also Merry 1988: 872 on the division between classic and new legal pluralisms; Rouland 1994: 50-65; Berman 2007.

The question is whether a ruling separated from its context is meaningless without the decision making process, as claimed by the critics of restatements? Or whether the glorification of the process is simply essentialism? Should one not record the rules, if there is a state legal system after all? The answer given by Schiller was to make the traditional rules as compiled earlier by the traditional authorities available, and to enable the indigenous people itself to develop its own rules. However, the end result in this case was a victory for deep pluralism as described by Schiller in his article on Coptic law in Late Antiquity: the abandonment of the state legal system.

Conclusions

In recent years scholarship has increasingly recognized the often scientifically guided efforts that colonial powers made to further the development of their African colonies. It has been noted that the simplistic picture of colonialism as oppression and ignorance is not perhaps the most accurate but more the product of emancipatory postcolonial scholarship, which drew a strict separation between the enlightened and the oppressive. In practice the problems were too complex to be resolved simply by good will (Cooper 2004: 9-38).

There were two conflicting agendas for legal reform in Ethiopia and Africa in general: modernization through the adoption of legislation after Western models, and the reform and renewal of traditional African law. The Ethiopian imperial government sought to modernize society through legislation, while Schiller attempted to demonstrate the wisdom of the latter. In the end, both projects were made redundant by the socialist revolution. However, the intellectual history of legal reforms would be incomplete without both, because they testify to the alternatives considered and the process of the struggle for legal reform.

While colonial powers had imposed their own laws on their African colonies, the main consideration in African legal reforms was the restatement of customary law. Indigenous law was applied in courts already during the colonial period, but the issue of deducing the content of that law remained. The bulk of the legal systems in Africa were normally the imported laws of the colonial state, which was reflected in the aims of legal reforms. On the one hand, restatements of African customary laws were made and, on the other, law schools were founded to train African professionals who would master the legal system left behind by the colonizers. African nationalists had mixed feelings with both elements of the legal system: the European law was an imposed, alien system, but customary law had also been a tool of colonialism.

The project of Schiller was based on the premise that legal pluralism was the future of African law. The Ethiopian Civil Law codification recognized a very limited validity of customary law in the norms of land tenure, which Schiller used as a pretext for his project. The project also had a wider agenda, demonstrating that law reform based on the utilization of traditional law was possible and would successfully correct the nullification of law in rural areas.

As one of the pioneers of the study of African law in the United States, Schiller could utilize his network of connections within the African law community. Though the law school at Addis Ababa was committed to modernization and law reform, former students and colleagues from the African Law Center he had founded at Columbia University would assist him in the process. Schiller's background was in the historical study of legal pluralism and as such his approach to legal reform was very different from that of the young modernizers of the law faculty. In his studies on ancient Egyptian Coptic law and Indonesian *Adat* law, Schiller was committed to the primary nature of indigenous law in legal pluralism.

However, Schiller was hindered by the quest for historical accuracy and originality, the search for early and uncontaminated sources. As in the nineteenth century German law reform, with which Schiller was intimately familiar, the result was not a record of a living tradition but rather an antiquarian exercise. The fundamentals of the process were flawed, and the decline of Ethiopia into revolution and later civil war ended the project before corrective measures could be taken.

The legacy of Schiller is in legal pluralism, where he attempted to chart a course between the subjection of indigenous law to the state legal system and its irrelevance. The colonial state legal pluralism recognized indigenous law only as a set of rules, while the contemporary idea of deep legal pluralism attempts to take into account indigenous law but considers its existence independent of state structures. Schiller was unashamedly state centered and held that in order to be relevant in practice, the rules of indigenous law should be developed and reformed. A lawyer and thinking like one, he saw little utility in the detachment of indigenous law and the state. Even though African nationalists intent on development saw customary law as unchangeable and beyond reform and political control, Schiller advocated autonomy and development within the traditional culture.

References

ALLOTT, Antony N.

1957 'The Judicial Ascertainment of Customary Law in British Africa.' *Modern Law Review* 20: 244-263.

1970 *New Essays in African* Law, London: Butterworths.

1987 'Introduction', Pp. xi-xv in Eugene Cotran, *Case Book on Kenya Customary Law.* Abingdon and Nairobi: Professional Books and Nairobi University Press.

ALLOTT, Antony N., A.L. EPSTEIN, and Max GLUCKMAN

1969 'Introduction.' Pp. 1-21 in Max Gluckman (ed.), *Ideas and Procedures in African Customary Law.* Oxford: Oxford University Press.

ALLOTT, Antony N. and Gordon R. WOODMAN (eds.)

1985 *People's Law and State Law.* Dordrecht: Foris.

ANDERSON, J.N.D.

1954 *Islamic Law in Africa.* London: Colonial Office.

ASANTE, Samuel K.B.

1987 'Over a Hundred Years of a National Legal System in Ghana.' *Journal of African Law* 31: 70-92.

BENDA-BECKMANN, Franz von and Han F. VERMEULEN

2001 'Adat Law and Legal Anthropology: in memoriam Johan Frederik (Hans) Holleman; with a bibliography.' *Journal of Legal Pluralism* 46: 103-114.

BENNETT, Tom W.

2004 *Customary Law in South Africa.* Landsdowne: Juta.

2006 'Conflict of Laws.' Pp. 15-28 in J.C. Bekker, Christa Rautenbach and N.M.I. Goolam (eds.), *Introduction to Legal Pluralism in South Africa.* Durban: LexisNexis Butterworths.

2009 'Re-Introducing African Customary Law to the South African Legal System.' *American Journal of Comparative Law* 57: 1-32.

BENTON, Lauren

2002 *Law and Colonial Cultures: Legal Regimes in World History, 1400-1900.* New York: Cambridge University Press.

BERMAN, Paul Schiff

2007 'Global Legal Pluralism.' *Southern California Law Review* 80: 1155-1237.

BRIETZKE, Paul

1975 'Law and Rural Development in Ethiopia.' *African Studies Review* 18: 45-62.

BURMAN, Sandra and Wilfried SCHÄRF
1990 'Creating People's Justice: Street Committees and People's Courts in a South African City.' *Law & Society Review* 24: 693-744.
CHANOCK, Martin
1985 *Law, Custom, and Social Order: The Colonial Experience in Malawi and Zambia*. Cambridge: Cambridge University Press.
1991 'Law, State and Culture: Thinking About "Customary Law" After Apartheid.' *Acta Juridica* 1991: 52-70.
1996 'The South African Native Administration Act of 1927: Reflections on a Pathological Case of Legal Pluralism.' Pp. 295-323 in Oliver Mendelsohn and Upendra Baxi (eds.), *The Rights of Subordinated Peoples*. Delhi: Oxford University Press.
2001 *The Making of South African Legal Culture 1902-1936: Fear, Favour and Prejudice*. Cambridge: Cambridge University Press.
COOPER, Frederick
2004 'Development, Modernization, and the Social Sciences in the Era of Decolonization: The Examples of British and French Africa.' *Revue d'histoire des sciences humaines* 10: 9-38.
COTRAN, Eugene
1968 *Restatement of African Law: Volume 1. Kenya I, Marriage and Divorce*. London: Sweet and Maxwell.
1969 *Restatement of African Law: Volume 2, Kenya II, The Law of Succession*. London: Sweet and Maxwell.
1987 'Tony Allott, Pioneer of the Study of African Law: A Personal Memoir.' *Journal of African Law* 31: 15-17.
DAVID, René
1963 'A Civil Code for Ethiopia.' *Tulane Law Review* 37: 187-204.
1967 'Sources of the Ethiopian Civil Code.' *Journal of Ethiopian Law* 4: 431-349.
DAVIDSON, Jamie and David HENLEY (eds.)
2007 *The Revival of Tradition in Indonesian Politics: The Deployment of Adat from Colonialism to Indigenism*. Abingdon: Routledge.
ELIAS, T. Olawale
1956 *The Nature of African Customary Law*. Manchester: Manchester University Press.
FASSEUR, C.
1992 'Colonial Dilemma: Van Vollenhoven and the Struggle Between Adat Law and Western Law in Indonesia.' Pp. 239-256 in W. J. Mommsen and J. A. De Moor (eds.), *European Expansion and Law: The Encounter of European and Indigenous Law in 19th and 20th Century Africa and Asia.*

Oxford: Berg.

FAVALI, Lyda and Roy PATEMAN

2003 *Blood, Land, and Sex: Legal and Political Pluralism in Eritrea.* Bloomington: Indiana University Press.

GLUCKMAN, Max

1949 'Adat Law in Indonesia.' *Journal of Comparative Legislation and International Law* 31: 60-65.

GOLDIN, Bennie and Michael GELFAND

1975 *African Law and Custom in Rhodesia.* Cape Town: Juta & Co.

HAYDON, E.S.

1960 *Law and Justice in Buganda.* London: Butterworths.

HAILE SELLASSIE I

1964 'Inaugural Statement.' *Journal of Ethiopian Law* 1: v-vi.

HOEBEL, E. Adamson and A. Arthur SCHILLER

1948 'Introduction.' Pp. 1-43, in B. ter Haar, *Adat Law in Indonesia.* New York: Institute of Pacific Relations.

HOOKER, M. B.

1978 *Adat law in Modern Indonesia.* Kuala Lumpur and New York: Oxford University Press.

IBIK, J.O.

1970 *Restatement of African Law: Vol. 3. Malawi I, The Law of Marriage and Divorce.* London: Sweet and Maxwell 1970.

1971 *Restatement of African Law: Vol. 4. Malawi II, The Law of Land, Succession, Movable Property, Agreements and Civil Wrongs.* London: Sweet and Maxwell.

ILC (INTERNATIONAL LEGAL CENTER)

1974 *Law and Development: The Future of Law and Development Research.* Uppsala: International Legal Center.

1975 *Legal Education in a Changing World.* Uppsala: International Legal Center.

JOHNSTONE, Quintin

1971-1972 'American Assistance to African Legal Education.' *Tulane Law Review* 46: 657-723.

KIDANE, Mangisteab

1990 *Ethiopia. Failure of Land Reform and Agricultural Crisis: Contributions in Afro-American Studies.* New York: Greenwood Press.

KLUDZE, A.K.P.

1973 *Restatement of African Law: Vol 6. Ghana I, Ewe law of property.* London: Sweet and Maxwell.

KRZECTUNOWICZ, George
1966 'Turning the Legal Clock Back.' *Journal of Ethiopian Law* 3: 621-634.
KUPER, Hilda and Leo KUPER (eds.)
1965 *African Law: Adaptation and Development.* Berkeley and Los Angeles: University of California Press.
LEWIN, Julius
1938 'The Recognition of Native Law and Custom in British Africa.' *Journal of Comparative Legislation and International Law* 20: 16-23.
1947 *Studies in African Native Law.* Cape Town: The African Bookman.
MERRY, Sally
1988 'Legal Pluralism.' *Law & Society Review* 22: 869-896.
MOORE, Sally Falk
1992 'Treating Law as Knowledge: Telling Colonial Officers What to Say to Africans about Running "Their Own" Native Courts', *Law & Society Review* 26: 11-46.
NIEKERK, Gardiol van
2001 'State initiatives to incorporate non-state laws into the legal order: a denial of legal pluralism?' *Comparative and International Law Journal of Southern Africa* 34: 349-361.
2006 'Legal Pluralism.' Pp. 3-15, in J.C. Bekker Christa Rautenbach and N.M.I. Goolam (eds.), *Introduction to Legal Pluralism in South Africa.* Durban: LexisNexis Butterworths.
NKRUMAH, Kwame
1962 'Ghana - Law in Africa, Legal Education in Africa.' *Journal of African Law* 6: 103-108.
PAUL, James C.N.
1962-1963 'Legal Education in English-Speaking Africa.' *Journal of Legal Education* 15: 189-204.
1967 'Fourth Annual Report of the Dean.' *Journal of Ethiopian Law* 4: 21-31.
1987 'American Law Teachers and Africa.' *Journal of African Law* 31: 18-28.
PETERS, Pauline
2009 'Challenges in Land Tenure and Land Reform in Africa: Anthropological Contributions.' *World Development* 37: 1317–1325.
QUINLAN, Tim
1988 'The Perpetuation of Myths: A Case Study on 'Tribe' and 'Chief' in South Africa.' *Journal of Legal Pluralism* 27: 79-115.
READ, James S.
1987 'Tony Allott: A Colleague's Tribute.' *Journal of African Law* 31: 3-14.

REYNTJENS, Filip
1992 'The Development of the Dual Legal System in Former Belgian Central Africa (Zaire-Rwanda-Burundi).' Pp. 111-127 in W. J. Mommsen and J. A. De Moor (eds.), *European Expansion and Law: The Encounter of European and Indigenous Law in 19th and 20th Century Africa and Asia.* Oxford: Berg.

RIJKSUNIVERSITEIT TE LEIDEN
1956 *The Future of Customary Law in Africa: Symposium-Colloque Amsterdam, 1955.* Leiden: Universitaire Pers Leiden.

ROBERTS, Richard and Kristin MANN
1991 'Introduction.' Pp. 3-60 in Richard Roberts and Kristin Mann (eds.), *Law in Colonial Africa.* Portsmouth: Heinemann.

ROBERTS, Simon
1972 *Restatement of African Law: Vol. 5. Botswana I, Tswana Family Law.* London: Sweet and Maxwell.

ROULAND, Norbert
1994 *Legal Anthropology* (transl. P. G. Planel). Stanford: Stanford University Press.

SALACUSE, Jeswald W.
1975 *An Introduction to Law in French-Speaking Africa I-II.* Charlottesville: Michie.

SAND, Peter H.
2009 'Review of Heinrich Scholler, *Recht und Politik in Äthiopien: Von der traditionellen Monarchie zum modernen Staat* (LIT Verlag, 2008).' *American Journal of Comparative Law* 57: 754-762.

SCHAPERA, Ian
1938 *A Handbook of Tswana Law and Custom.* Oxford: Oxford University Press.

SCHILLER, A. Arthur
1932 *Ten Coptic Legal Texts.* New York: The Metropolitan Museum of Art.
1936 'Native Customary Law in the Netherlands East Indies.' *Pacific Affairs* 2: 254-263.
1942 'Conflict of Laws in Indonesia.' *The Far Eastern Quarterly* 2: 31-47.
1960 'Brussels Colloquium on the Recording of Customary Law.' *Journal of African Law* 4: 65.
1962 'Conflict of Laws in East Africa.' Pp. 430-454 in *De conflictu legum: Essays presented to Roeland Duco Kollewijn [and] Johannes Offerhaus at their seventieth birthdays, collected by the editors of the Netherlands International Law Review.* Leiden: A.W. Sijthoff.

1966 'Law and Society: Africa; Legal Aspects of a Developing Society.' *Wisconsin Law Review* 1966: 996-998.

1969 'Customary Land Tenure among the Highland Peoples of Northern Ethiopia: A Bibliographical Essay.' *African Law Studies* 1: 1-22.

1971 'The Courts are No More.' Pp. 469-502 in *Studi in onore di Eduardo Volterra, vol. 1.*, Milano: Giuffrè.

1978 *Roman Law: Mechanisms of Development.* The Hague and New York: Mouton.

SHADLE, Brett L.

1999 'Changing Traditions to Meet Current Altering Conditions: Customary Law, African Courts and the Rejection of Codification in Kenya, 1930-60.' *The Journal of African History* 40: 411-431.

SINGER, Norman J.

2008 'The Early Days of the Faculty of Law, AAU.' *Mizan Law Review* 2: 137-145.

TAMANAHA, Brian Z.

2008 'Understanding Legal Pluralism: Past to Present, Local to Global.' *Sydney Law Review* 30: 375-411.

TWINING, William

2010 'Normative and Legal Pluralism: A Global Perspective.' *Duke Journal of Comparative and International Law* 20: 473-517.

VANDERLINDEN, Jacques

1966 'A Further Note on an Introduction to the Sources of Ethiopian Law.' *Journal of Ethiopian Law* 3: 635-644.

WHITMAN, James

1990 *The Legacy of Roman Law in the German Romantic Era.* Princeton: Princeton University Press.

WOODMAN, Gordon R.

1969 'Some Realism About Customary Law – The West African Experience.' *Wisconsin Law Review* 1969: 128-152.

WOODMAN, Gordon R. and A.O. OBILADE (eds.)

1995 *African Law and Legal Theory.* New York: New York University Press.

THE INSIDERS AND THE OUTSIDERS: STANDARDIZATION AND 'FAILED' PERSON-MAKING IN A LITHUANIAN MARKET PLACE[1]

Ida Harboe Knudsen

As Lithuania entered the EU in 2004 together with nine other new member countries, agricultural producers met new laws and standards for production. The new standard regime proved to be a particular challenge for small scale farmers who hitherto had derived the main part of their income from the sale of raw milk products, and who now had to submit to a different set of regulations for production. During my fieldwork among small scale farmers in the Southwest of Lithuania, my attention was drawn to a peculiar effect of the new standards regime at the market place, where the women from my field site went every Saturday to sell their dairy products. Many of the women, who previously had enjoyed the privilege of selling inside the market hall among other certificated farmers, lost their right to sell their milk and cheese as they could not fulfil the EU regulations. Because they could not afford to lose the income from the sale of dairy products, they did not withdraw from commercial production as demanded, but instead started selling illegally outside the bounds of the market.[2] In my field notes I

[1] This article is based on fieldwork carried out in Lithuania in 2006-2007. The research has been financed by the EU through the Marie Curie SocAnth Programme in cooperation with the Max Planck Institute for Social Anthropology in Halle, Germany.

[2] I carried out fieldwork in the market place in Marijampolė both during my first

referred to the two groups of salespeople at the Lithuanian market place as *the Insiders* and *the Outsiders*. I intended the double meaning. The Insiders were both as a matter of fact placed inside, within the market hall, and they were also legally placed within the realm of EU legal orders. This is in contrast to the Outsiders, who were placed on the other side of the market bounds and sold products outside the realm of EU legal orders.

The manipulation of space as vividly displayed by the Outsiders posed problems at the market place as it invited ridicule of the authorities and displayed the shortcomings of EU law on the local level. It appeared that, although all production now was subject to the new EU-regulations, the actual enforcement of law was only practised within certain spaces which could be controlled, and on producers who from the onset had an interest in being controlled. What intrigued me about the Insider/Outsider situation in the market place was that this was not a case of homemade products versus products from the store, but a case of essentially similar products, which have ended up on both sides of the law, after a process which has resulted in a re-location of people and a re-evaluation of products and producers in the light of the EU-standard regime.

In her research Elizabeth Dunn suggests that a close link is established between the implementation of standards and the 'making' of a specific kind of (EU) person (Dunn 2005). In this article I suggest that the shortcomings of law at the Lithuanian market place are closely connected with what I with reference to Dunn refer to as a 'failed' person-making. By this it is to be understood that the 'making' of such producers is challenged by the local actors' understanding and negotiations of the rules. Rather than adapting to a rating according to EU standards, they seek to optimize their possibilities either within or outside the boundaries of the law. This is closely connected with a 'failed' making of the customer. Indeed, as long as Lithuanians favour the 'authentic' Lithuanian product, the EU-standard regime and its measurement of product quality will face intense competition by small scale (illegal) producers.

---

stay in Lithuania from January to July 2004 and again during my second stay from October 2006 to October 2007. I am thus able to draw on field data from both periods of research.

Research and Field Site

This article is based on one and a half years' research, in two parts. My first fieldwork lasted six months and was conducted in a village in the Southwest of Lithuania in the months just before and after the official entry into the EU on 1 May 1, 2004. For the second part I returned in 2006-2007 to conduct a longer research into the impact which EU-membership had had on the Lithuanian agricultural sector. My participant observation took place both among Insiders and Outsiders at the market place, and in the village, where I followed and participated in the production of dairy products, from the milking of the cows up to the point at which the final product was ready to go to the market, whether outside or inside the hall. I furthermore conducted informal interviews with customers at the market place and paid frequent trips to the bigger cities to meet with agricultural experts.

Enlargement Through Compatibility

The Insider/Outsider conflict is related to the great enlargement of the EU in 2004, when the union grew from 15 to 25 member states, and its total population grew by almost 75 million people to about 450 million. The acceptance of more members into the EU was a challenge for the agricultural sector as the market for agricultural products necessarily changed when 10 new members came onto the stage (Wallace 2000). In order to integrate the agricultural production of the new member states into the overall production of the EU, the new states were required to meet specific standards for food production and food processing as detailed in the *Acquis Communautaire* (the entire body of EU law). This meant that products from the new member states were expected to become the same as those of their Western European counterparts (Bellier and Wilson 2000). This, according to Andrew Barry, concerned the creation of a specific technical form as the trademark of the EU (Barry 2001). The EU requirements are part of the central process of *harmonization* of products within the EU, which implies that products and their manufacture are to be governed by the same legislation in all member countries, according to a 'one size fits all' model. The problem arose in the new member countries that the methods of production of small scale producers was from the onset too different to be encapsulated in the EU-regime of standards and quality, and there was little or no chances of making them compatible with that regime as people lacked the necessary resources and knowledge. The outcome was that, when EU-laws were imposed on small-scale production, much of what hitherto had been occurring inside the boundaries of the law was now classified as illegal (Dunn 2005; Caldwell 2009; Harboe Knudsen 2010).

In Lithuania awareness of the new standards regime was raised through countless agricultural meetings and seminars open to all farmers, by emphasizing the advisory role of the local agricultural consultants, through media, through the distribution of folders and leaflets about EU-requirements, and simply by changes in the laws regulating production. The Lithuanian Farmers' Union (*Lietuvos Ūkininkų Sąjunga*, LŪS) arranged various seminars taught by professors from the Agricultural University in Kaunas, lawyers, and agricultural advisors. The idea behind this was to re-educate those farmers who had the knowledge and resources and were of such an age to be able to change production, and to encourage farmers who could not comply with the new standard regime to withdraw from production altogether.

About Standards and Persons

Elizabeth Dunn has discussed the effect of standardization policy using the example of a Polish meatpacking company (Dunn 2005). She argues that the implementation of standards leads to a making of persons: workers are transformed into obedient, self-disciplining citizens who internalize the system of EU-values and thereby come to self-control their working process (Dunn 2005; see also: Dunn 2003, 2004). In the farming sector this plays out by the farmers who can comply with EU-standards coming to be included, while those who no longer have permission to produce being forced to withdraw to a socialist mode of production and thereby a socialist personhood as they now engage in sale outside the legal framework (Dunn 2005). Diana Mincyte, in her study of the informal sale of dairy products in Lithuania, evokes a somewhat different argument. Based on her own research she suggests that the women engaged in illegal sale (Outsiders in my vocabulary) create a niche in the EU-regime where they can gain economic and social capital: they claim their own space and engage in informal production as capable and autonomous agents (Mincyte 2009). Based on my ethnographic material I would argue for an understanding which balances the idea of the obedient subject with that of the autonomous agent. Here I draw on Giddens, who emphasizes the duality of structures, meaning by this that structures shape human behaviour and human behaviour also shapes and reproduces structures (Giddens 2003). This approach also leads to a more careful elaboration of the extent to which people can or will act in the face of structures: agency is far from uniform, varying a great deal in both kind and extent (Sewell 1992).

In my approach structure and actors are bound together in an inter-related dynamic of options and limitations by engagement in what I call practical negotiation in everyday life within the given structure. Thus a person might find herself in a situation in which she on the one hand is unable to do what is expected of her, but on the other hand needs to maintain everyday life. She cannot, or will not, follow the rules strictly, but neither can she - or maybe will she - avoid the situation altogether. Instead she develops an intermediate strategy in order to keep going. She is then not necessarily resisting these structures, but rather merely trying to find a way in between what is required and what is possible. As a result normative constellations and socio-economic and shifting laws continue to influence people's decisions. This balance between structure and actions should be seen in relation to my conceptualization of law. Law is not limited to formal laws such as state law or EU law, but applies to different constellations of normative orders in society. In this sense, law becomes an umbrella term for different orders and regulations (F. von Benda-Beckmann 1997; F. and K. von Benda-Beckmann 2006). This also complies with the analysis of Moore, who works from the viewpoint which holds that law is not above society. Her viewpoint is close to that of Ehrlich, when she states that law should not be condensed into one term, abstracted from the social context in which it exists (cf. Ehrlich 1936). Law and the social context in which it operates must be examined together.[3] This approach not only takes into consideration 'formal' law, but also aims at understanding how other (unwritten) local norms of behaviour may influence people's decisions and regulate their behaviour, even those normative rules of behaviour which contradict official law. In this regard I propose that, because the Insiders and the Outsiders must continually consider the different constellations of their everyday life - official law, informal normative orders, the economic situation of the family, customers' willingness to buy outside the market hall, the inefficient legal control outside the market bounds, etc. – EU law is but one out of many (legal and normative) factors they must take into consideration.

The Insiders and the Outsiders

The Market

The market hall is a quite ugly building made of grey metallic plates, appearing

[3] Ehrlich drew a distinction between what he called state law, and living law, where state law referred to the rules of society, and living law was the social reality in which the subjects were engaged (Ehrlich 2002).

like a hangar hovering in the centre of the market place. It is located in the centre of the seventh largest city in Lithuania, Marijampolė, which has approximately 50,000 inhabitants. Looking at the market hall from the outside, nothing tells you that this is one of the liveliest markets in Marijampolė. Starting at 7a.m., sellers are at their stalls with a variety of food products. Large numbers of people circulate. Regular customers normally buy from the same person every time, others prefer to go through all the products and visit every stall in order to be sure that they get the best quality at the best price. Seen from the main entrance, the section on the right is mostly for different meat products, such as a wide variety of sausages and smoked or salted pork. The left side is partly for fish sales and partly for processed (as distinct from homemade) food. The stalls in the centre are occupied by farmers selling honey, covering all forms from light green to deep yellow depending on the flowers from which the bees have gathered it. The other stalls in the middle are occupied by farmer-women selling their homemade dairy products. The most popular product in this section is *grietinė*, which is similar to sour cream, but much thicker and sweeter. The women keep it in big buckets, and when customers come the women dip in big spoon, lift it up and let the *grietinė* run down into the bucket again. In this way the customers can see how thick it is. The Lithuanian white compressed egg-shaped cheese (*baltas sūris*) is also a valued product, as is the *varškė,* curd packed in small plastic bags. A few of the women also sell unprocessed milk in two-litre bottles. These bottles are typically used cola, lemonade or beer bottles which the sellers clean and recycle as milk bottles. All products are kept in open cooling boxes in front of the women, securing that they are kept at the right temperature[4].

The open air market outside is characterized by random sale of non-food and food products (but not dairy products) in what appears as an untidy mixture. Here you can get everything from home-knitted woollen socks to shoes, old books and journals, imported Byelorussian clothes laid out on the ground, vegetables, fruits and berries, technical equipment, big spoons and forks cut from wood, cheap cosmetics and perfumes, small prayer books, painted pictures with romantic and/or religious motifs, used plastic bags from Western European stores, blankets, flower- and vegetable seeds, and many, many other goods.

A third sales space is located beyond the open-air market. Just on the other side of the almost invisible sign marking the boundary of the market is a row of elderly

[4] The cooling boxes came into the market place after entry into the EU in 2004. Prior to that, the women had simply had their products on a table.

women. In front of them on the ground are baskets with white cheese and *varškė*, big milk bottles and buckets with *grietinė*, the very same products which are sold inside. The location is cleverly chosen. Being just outside the market bounds, the authorities of the market place cannot claim control over the products nor fees for their sale. Nevertheless, every customer who wishes to enter the market from the main street will pass the row of Outsiders first, which gives everybody an opportunity to buy their dairy products here at a cheaper price.

Inside the Market; Rising Expenses, Rising Prices

The women inside the market hall mostly come from relatively small households with a few cows, often leading a better life than the majority of the villagers and viewing themselves as decent, law-abiding citizens. They have calculated that delivering unprocessed milk to the dairy is unprofitable. Instead they can make money by selling homemade dairy products at the market. In order to fulfil the criteria enforced within the market hall, they need to have a better than average knowledge of milk production and hygiene and be able to invest in equipment which complies with the requirements. It was at this market, inside the market hall, that two of my informants from the village of Straigiai, Asta and Stasė, sold their dairy products. Asta is in her late thirties, and lives with her parents, her husband and their two children in the village where they work on Asta's parents' 11-hectare farm. Stasė is in her mid sixties and also lives in the village together with her husband, and runs a farm of 10 hectares.

Asta's *grietinė* was by far the most popular in the market hall. It was very thick and sweet. Most customers only bought from Stasė or the other women when Asta had sold out. However, Stasė's cheese was more highly valued than Asta's cheese. As all the fat from Asta's milk went into the production of *grietinė,* the remaining milk that she used for cheese was very light. As Stasė did not separate milk from cream so carefully, the milk she used for cheese was fatter. Stasė also took extra time to make the popular sweet white cheese with eggs, sugar, and raisins. This was her little specialty, which enabled her to compensate for her less popular *grietinė*. If the cheese is not fat, the women told me, it does not have any substance, and you have to sell it at a lower price. The women laughed and shook their heads when I told them that in my country people often pay more for low-fat dairy products, because they wanted to stay slim.

The families of Asta and Stasė had, along with the other Insiders, official permission to sell their dairy products. Their animals had been thoroughly checked by veterinarians, their products were tested and controlled, the production facilities were carefully checked, and the women paid 6 *litas* (1.74 euro) to the market hall administration every Saturday when they came with their produce baskets. Within the hall products were also controlled by a system of random testing. At the market place, a woman with two cows could make about 480 *litas* (139 euro) a month in the winter and up to 580 *litas* (168 euro) in the summer, when the cows give more milk. An average state pension in 2007 was about 600 *litas* (174 euro), so, selling at the market place produced a much-needed extra income. However, as the costs of production grew with the EU, it became quite expensive to sell products at the market. Consequently, the women had to sell their products at higher prices. As prices rose customers grew dissatisfied. People went to the market place expecting to get a good deal, that is, to buy fresh products at low prices. Customers now realized that the price level in the market hall came dangerously close to that in the grocery stores. A cheese which prior to EU entry had cost 3 *litas* (0.87 euro) cost 5 *litas* (1.45 euro) at the time of my fieldwork, *varškė* was being sold for 3.5 *litas* a bag (1 euro) in comparison to the previous 2.5 *litas* (0.72 euro). This price example is valid also for half a litre of *grietinė*. Sometimes there was no longer any difference between prices at the market and in the grocery stores, which affected especially pensioners who had to count every *litas* they had, and who hitherto had saved a great deal of money by buying market products. Many a dissatisfied customer now turned away from the women inside with the remark "it is the same as in the stores" (*tas pats parduotuvėse*), meaning, there was no longer money to be saved by purchasing products in the market hall. Sometimes the Insiders would have to return home with several cheeses and litres of milk that did not sell. The customers they lost were those who could no longer afford to buy inside the market hall. However, those who stayed despite the rising prices were those who valued the fact that the products were controlled. It was not unusual for customers who bought inside to ask about the dairy product, how it was made and if it was safe to eat. "You see" Asta once said to me, after a well dressed woman had inquired about the cheese and the certificate before she had finally bought it, "people do care in here; they want to know what they buy. We can provide that guarantee for them."[5]

Outside the Market: Enduring the Weather

Whereas it would be the same people trading inside the market hall every week,

[5] From my field notes, February 2007.

the group of Outsiders was not as consistent. Some women were regulars, others only came from time to time. Sometimes there would be few traders outside, other times many, the number ranging from five to 13, whereas there were six Insiders. One sure indicator of the number of Outsiders on a given Saturday would be the weather. Indeed, I found a simple but reliable rule for the market: the worse the weather, the fewer the women trading outside. Trading outside was tough. If it rained they had to protect their products from the weather, if it was freezing, there was the danger that the cheese and *grietinė* would also freeze, which would make them less attractive to customers. In the summer period, however, it was best to sell the products as early in the morning as possible, as it was not advisable to keep the dairy products outside in the hot sun for a long time. The weather conditions were the main challenge the Outsiders faced, and was, indeed, much worse than the rare intervention by a police officer coming and sending them away.

While the weather often turned out to be an obstacle for them, the Outsiders benefited from their location in front of the market and from their low prices. The Outsiders did not have the necessary money to improve their facilities at home, to send products for bacteriological tests, or to pay for a stall inside. Consequently they could not move inside. However, because they had no fees to pay, they could cut their prices and sell their products at prices anywhere between one and three *litas* cheaper than inside. A woman who sold outside explained:

> Just as the women inside have their [regular] customers; we have ours [...]. I have people who come to me every time I am here [...], they see that my cheese looks good, they eat it and see that my cheese is tasty, fat, and healthy. So they come back to me next week. Why should they pay twice the price inside?[6]

Two of the women had only joined the Outsiders in 2004 when they lost their permission to sell inside the market. There were others who had lost their permission, too, they said, but had instead chosen to sell to friends and neighbours instead of standing outside the market hall. The women who were selling outside could not freely choose their space; they only had the option of outside sale. Whereas Insiders could become Outsiders, Outsiders never became Insiders.

[6] Interview, March 2007.

Changing Spaces, Challenging Laws

In studies about market places in post-socialist countries, it has been noted how officially approved markets and dubious semi-legal markets are separated from each other through spatial distinctions. What is interesting in this regard is that this distance from one another appears to be significant. Hence, we may have the approved market in the city, and the contested market several kilometres outside the city (Smigielska 1992; Hohnen 2003; Dunn, 2005; Humphrey and Skvirskaja 2009). As Humphrey and Skvirskaja suggest, based on their study of a semi-legal Ukrainian container market, "[...] any city needs (or allows to be created) a notional space of 'outside' [...]" (Humphrey and Skvirskaja 2009: 64). In Marijampolė this space of 'outside' is created inside the city. The distinctive feature of this market place is thus not the illegal selling in itself, as it takes place in various locations in Lithuania (and in other post-socialist countries), but that the legally approved and legally disapproved markets are just next to one another. The Outsiders use location and space to circumvent rules, as they benefit from the flow of customers who have to pass the Outsiders in order to enter the market inside. This use of space both demonstrates the strength of EU law (ensuring strict enforcement inside) and proves the limitations of EU law (allowing the lack of enforcement of law outside the official territory). An agricultural advisor commented on the situation: "The market is controlled and exclusive for those farmers who produce according to the rules. But then people just sell outside the market. And that is difficult to control, very difficult. Because what are you supposed to do? Go and visit every grandmother in Lithuania and tell her to stop selling milk?"[7]

The competition from outside caused the Insiders distress, especially on the days when they had to return home with unsold dairy products because the customers had bought outside. This led to an ambiguous relationship to the Outsiders, as they were partly looked down upon, partly cursed, partly envied for their go-around-the-rules strategies. Stasė told me:

> We were very dissatisfied. The question [of illegal sales] was raised many times. I always asked: "are we a bad kind of people, since we are treated worse than them [the Outsiders]?" We had to meet all requirements, do all the tests, pay for everything, and pay for selling at the market. [...] We also raised the questions at

[7] Interview, Kaunas municipal administration, November 2006.

> meetings but no one was interested. We called the police. The officers came and told the women to go home. As soon as the officers left, the old *močiutes* (grandmothers, elderly women) came back.[8]

The question of the Outsiders came down to a matter of space and interpretation of space. 'Inside' and 'outside' were clearly bounded and concrete physical spaces, but they were imbedded with different meanings and subjects for different interpretations of law. The law was negotiated through a clever play with space, which in the end outdid the actual legislation. As F and K von Benda-Beckmann argue, "spatial constructions as embodied in legal categories and regulation provide sets of resources that become part of 'spatial idiom-shopping' [...]" (F and K von Benda-Beckmann 2009: 116). What the Outsiders did was to use the options they had within the limitations the law imposed on them. The notions of physical, social, and legal space can be seen as interacting phenomena, such that the bounded space governed by law influences interaction. Likewise do the law and its (spatial) limitations provide resources for people, making them capable of pursuing their own (economic, political) interests within the given space (F and K von Benda-Beckmann 2009).

The Outsiders turned their exclusion from the market into a benefit by creating a 'non-EU space'. The non-EU space was a normative construction, a circumvention of rules as a response to their exclusion from the market, and was mobilized against the inside market as a way for the Outsiders to meet their economic goals. It was, as I frame it, a practical negotiation of the situation. The fact that the women stood outside the market did not legalize their sale, it only meant that the market administration could not interfere. The only thing the administration could do was to put up notes and posters inside the market hall emphasizing that they had no responsibility for food products sold outside the market. Alternatively, the problem was passed on to the police, who had a legal right to move the women from their spot. However, the calls from the Insiders to the police in the end resulted in relatively few visits by the police officers. Indeed, on the general crime-scale in Marijampole, removing elderly women from the market, just for them to return to it as soon as the officers leave, is not on the top of their list on combating crime. Even *if* the police had been consistent in removing the old women, it would only be the tip of the iceberg since most outsider sales took place in disguise. Products were also sold from cars after dark (referred to as 'car-boot

[8] Interview, May 2007.

sales': Pine 2001), or by old women on bicycles. In Marijampolė, the urban yards were divided into different territories shared by a number of Outsiders, who would have their own yards to which they came twice a week with their dairy products. There was also the option of selling products to neighbours and friends, all practices which classify as outsider trade, as the products were not officially approved. Hence, most Outsiders are doing their sales in spaces very distinct from the market place. It appeared that EU product control mainly worked for those who were already imbedded in the system while the controls did not reach the groups of people who, according to the law, were the most obvious targets for legal intervention.

Senses of Personhood

Practical Negotiations Among Insiders

The new standard regime led to new conceptualizations of both the products and their producers. Insiders reproduced EUropean rhetoric in order to appear economically, socially, and morally superior to the disadvantageous Outsiders. Although there were plenty of privileges obtained through exclusion, the Insiders connected legality with a certain pride. Being inside was thus both the state of being imbedded in the EUropean trading system and a way to receive symbolic capital in terms of recognition and respect. It was also a way to distinguish oneself from the Outsiders and, thus, define oneself as a person in accordance with both the EU and the local environment. This was exemplified in their view of the Outsiders whom they saw as *prasti žmonės* (simple folks, lower class people) with little or no education. Asta, for one example, was the daughter of the previous agronomist of the collective farm in Straigiai, and it was certain that her father would never allow her to change space and stay with the 'dubious' women in front of the market. Likewise Stasė, also coming from one of the richer families, valued her reputation as a law-abiding citizen and an eager and devoted churchgoer. She was often acquiring new leaflets about the EU made it a matter of honour to know about the latest production requirements and options for funding and programme.

However, the longer I stayed with the women in the market hall, the more it seemed to me that the ideas of personhood and the borders between acceptable and non-acceptable actions were under steady negotiation. Whether or not the women subscribed to law was highly dependent on circumstances and possibilities. The women were not only in the market hall as salespeople, but they also bought products at the market. These were partly grocery products from the other stalls but also were products sold illegally within the market hall. This was especially true for illegally imported Byelorussian alcohol or cigarettes. This kind of sale contested the claim of the inside market to be legally "pure". Ragged looking men, dressed in big worn-out coats under which they hid a couple of plastic bags, would approach the Insiders discreetly at their stalls. The mutual understanding of the meeting was clear from this very starting point. The exchange of money and products was surprisingly quick, a nod in the right manner and a bottle and a carton of cigarettes would be in the women's baskets, where they hid it under a piece of cloth. When asking about the men selling these products, I was never given much of an answer. "Uh, he is such a... he is some bum (*bomžas*) smuggling and selling illegally, we do not talk with him," Stasė once said after having bought goods from a man.[9] While she distanced herself from the man by considering him as 'lower class' (bum), and his actions as 'bad' (smuggling and selling illegally), she still bought his products, quickly and in disguise. Hence, she claimed, she had nothing to do with the man as such, and did not wish to either. The 'bum' was surrounded by contrasting feelings of disgust and immorality, yet still desire for his products. Whereas I knew the women liked to drink although they would always deny it, the cigarettes puzzled me, as none of them smoked. Stasė had always talked about smoking as being a bad habit of poor people. "Why did you buy cigarettes from him?" I once asked her, "neither you nor your husband smoke." "Indeed we do not!" Stasė answered, "and we never did!" "But why did you buy them, then?" I asked, insisting on some kind of an answer. Stasė waited a moment and replied: "Well, there is this man living down the street, not far from our house and he sometimes comes and helps a bit at the farm. Then I pay him with cigarettes."[10]

Indeed, by re-circulating the illegal goods into the familiar sphere of networking, these goods lose their formerly ambiguous status. Other things were also kept behind the counter. The women often brought baskets along from home with food and alcohol, preferably vodka. While selling, the women would offer each other bread with cheese or meat, sweets, and alcohol. They always brought a single shot glass along, which was repeatedly filled with vodka and passed around from the very moment they started to sell to the moment they left for home. Drinking was something they otherwise verbally rejected as the path to all evil, but here it underwent a different discourse. Drinking was a way to keep warm during the cold

[9] From my field notes, February 2007.

[10] From my field notes, February 2007.

winter days in the market. To return home from the market place tipsy or even drunk was nothing exceptional. Although they distanced themselves from the Outsiders' sales, the Insiders' buying of illegally imported products was understood within a frame of practicalities and re-integrated into an accepted social sphere through common friendly consumption (alcohol) or redistribution in the wider household economy (cigarettes.) The norms they adhered to were not a simplified matter of right or wrong. Rather one model of behaviour would be disregarded in one context and accepted in another. The proclaimed borders between inside and outside the law were not ultimate and permanently fixed all.

This capacity for renegotiating the situation and sense of personhood became clear to me as both Asta and Stasė withdrew from the market hall. The reason for this was that both of their families had applied to take part in the EU's "Early Retirement Programme" which was offered to farmers above 55 (in the case of Asta, the retirement being granted to her father, in the case of Stasė, to her husband.) The aim of the programme was to reduce the number of small scale producers, by paying them to withdraw from production. They were allowed to keep one cow and two hectares of land and produce for their own consumption solely. Accepting this programme also meant that none of the women could keep their position inside the market hall, as this would have been a violation of the rules. Indeed, a few weeks after Stasė had obtained early retirement and was thus prohibited from selling her dairy products, I found her in the row of Outsiders she had previously looked down on. In her new renegotiation of the situation she, like the other Outsiders, turned exclusion into an economic benefit, by profiting from inflation and rising prices within the market hall. Hence, Insiders also had to make a daily living and, when pushed, to renegotiate their legal status. As Stasė explained: "The cow gives too much milk for me and my husband to consume alone, and who am I to waste it? Mind you, my products are still the same quality as before."[11]

As this example shows us: morality is cultivated with pride as long as people literally speaking can afford to have such standards. Asta herself never went outside the market hall to sell her products, and would refer to this as an option only jokingly. This did not mean that she stopped selling dairy products, but the sales were now to neighbours and other villagers, who would come to her house and ask for a cheese or a litre of milk. In principle, in the eyes of the EU this was no different than if she had actually moved outside the market hall. However, for

[11] Based on my field notes, May 2007.

Asta the difference was significant. She was not lined up with the Outsiders coming from God-only-knows what kind of farms, but had kept a safe and orderly place for sale: her home.

Reinventing the Cheese

Also for the Outsiders the changes brought about new awareness of the production facilities, pasteurization[12], hygiene, and bacteria. Dairy products produced under different circumstances were, viewed from the angle of the EU, potentially dangerous to consume. This challenged existing assumptions, as cheese that had been considered 'good quality' and 'safe to eat' prior to the entry into the EU was now suddenly viewed as 'low quality' and 'a danger to the health'. The emergence of this discourse does not mean that the Outsiders automatically adapted to it, but that they used it to gain a new understanding of their own products. One time I was having coffee with a few elderly women from the village of my research, the hostess encouraged me to cut a slice of the white cheese on the table and taste it. She carefully watched me while I was eating and now and then looked and nodded to the two neighbour women. As I had swallowed the last bit, she proudly and loudly exclaimed to her neighbours: "Did you see that? Ida eats my cheese! And she is from the EU [from an 'old' member state]. If it is good enough for her, then it is good for all EU-citizens!"[13] I, due to my Danish citizenship, now became a metonym for all consumers in the EU. Indeed, by referring to me as a 'sample' European, she overruled the so-called expert knowledge about cheese. In such ways people operated with ideas of the new standard regime and, in a somewhat counter-hegemonic way, turned perceptions around to the benefit of their own (non-certified) production. Indeed, the Outsiders now promoted their products as authentic and traditional, which in itself became a new agricultural fashion.

In a description of two competing French biscuit companies, Simon Roberts shows how a regional product is evoked by the conscious commercialization building on

[12] As the idea of pasteurization was introduced, people experimented with small portions, which were quickly heated in their microwaves before they could send them to the lab. There were, however, difficulties, as the glass or cup would burst in the microwave. The more common method was "slow pasteurization" where the milk would be standing in big pots on the stove and slowly reach the required 72-75 degrees Celsius.

[13] Based on my fieldnotes, May 2004.

(constructed) history, and only then becomes a product of heritage and tradition (Roberts 2007). Roberts is interested in the moment when the unspoken and previously taken for granted is made explicit. Thereby the product only gains its originality and heritage when it becomes part of a commercial discourse. Here, its authenticity as a traditional product becomes a prerequisite for its quality, and the present regains new meaning in the light of an idealized past (Roberts 2007). If we relate these thoughts to homemade food products from Lithuania such as the white cheese, we also follow a pattern by way of which it changes from being merely a cheese and becomes a consciously traditional Lithuanian product. The present understanding of the cheese as something distinct, original, and traditional, with an emphasis on the right shape and distinct taste, is created in comparison with 'synthetic' products imported from the West. As white cheese has never been imported, it gains specific substance in contrast to the other kinds of cheese, which now emerge at the market: various kinds of yellow cheese, cream cheese, camembert and even pre-sliced cheese, every slice being wrapped in plastic and ready to be put on toast. The synthetic versus the traditional is thus, I argue, related to a more complex understanding that goes far beyond cheese: the negative image of capitalism and a reflection of ambivalence toward the EU, as possibly representing a way to modernity, possibly a threat to the society due to 'fake' values. In the words of Roberts: "We are looking [....] at contemporary, self-conscious appeals to tradition in which elements of an exemplary, even idealized Arcadian past are explicitly evoked to form part of the life-world of the present." (Roberts, 2007: 27). The Lithuanian white cheese gained new ground in the meeting with the new discourse about food safety. It was no longer 'just' a cheese, it was, as I call it, the reinvention of the cheese as traditional, natural and distinct by its heritage.

Indeed, for the Outsiders it is also a question of competition with the Insiders, who essentially sell the same products, the difference only being that they are already legitimized as salespeople by the thorough tests of their milk. The evocation of the Outsiders' cheese as even *more* natural and *more* original than that of the Insiders was mobilized through a conscious mystification of the Insiders' products in the daily talk outside the market place. That the Insiders' products were now imbedded in the EU system would suggest that their products had been subjected to other forms for production, and consequently, that they were no longer selling the "original" products. The Outsiders, within their capability, thus furthered their claims to tradition and pure products. Looking at the Insiders' dairy products the production becomes an issue of control. People have to produce under new circumstances and are made aware of bacteria, hygiene, fat content, storage facilities, and animal nutrition, and the cheese is only accepted after having passed through bacteriological control. In this way, the means of production were changed, and the products standardized and 'improved'. Yet this possibly made it a somewhat different cheese than it originally was, not to mention, endowed with a mythical reality of EUropean impact giving body to stories spread by the Outsiders about the possibly damaging EUropeanization of production.

Making the Customer?

Wearing Europe, Ingesting Lithuania

Frances Pine, in a work about consumerism in Poland, has shown how the understanding of goods imported from the West has changed during the past decades. From being the status symbol of western culture during the socialist regime and thus in opposition to the socialist regime, the disappointments following the break-up of the Soviet Union made Western products the very symbol of betrayed hopes and promises (Pine 2001). The result was a turnaround in consumption, which took the form of the revival of national Polish products. In other words, Polish material culture and food products had a come-back, both as a way of voicing disappointment with the West, but also because many could simply not afford products imported from Western Europe (Pine 2001). In this way, consumption inevitably bears political connotations as an approval, or rejection, of changes and ideologies.

In the case of Lithuania, I found many mechanisms similar to what Pine remarked in her earlier work on Poland. The political, economic, and social ups and downs, however, had not resulted in a rejection of Western society by Lithuanians altogether. Many people in my field site were still fascinated with the west, had hope for increased wealth in the future, and aimed at adopting a modern and Western lifestyle (de Munck 2008). South American soap operas about beautiful and seductive (upper class) women and strong, handsome (and wealthy) men were among the favourite leisure time entertainments in the villages where I conducted research. Visiting the larger cities did not change this impression: going down the main shopping street in Kaunas, Laisvės Aleja, your attention is immediately drawn to the Lithuanian women with brightly bleached hair, shiny make-up, short skirts, and high boots, waltzing down the avenue (bound to make me feel hopelessly sloppy and out-of-fashion), mirroring the freedom to dress in what is considered a hip and modern fashion[14]. The same image of material fascination was conveyed through the many shopping malls which have been mushrooming all over Lithuania. However, the flawless façade could not embrace the many and often contradictory opinions and feelings people had about the changes in society. Co-existing with expectations or hopes for increased wealth was a fear of a moral degradation of Lithuania by the quick modernization of industry with low quality products as a result. And it embodied a set of negative images: 'fabrication' of animals and dairy products containing preservatives (Pine 2001; Caldwell 2009). If we relate these thoughts to the idea proposed by Pine, that consumption is an expression of approval or rejection of current politics and ideology, I suggest that the co-existing and contradictory feelings about the West have resulted in both a desire for and rejection of Western products. Indeed, the counter example to the consumption of (modern) Western style (non-food) products is seen at the food market. When people went to buy food here, it was in order *not* to buy imported products. Quite on the contrary, here they wanted what no import could outdo: '(home)made in Lithuania'. EU-rope was consumed with fancy 'outer' products, Lithuania with digestive 'inner' products.

Food Products and Conflicting Perceptions

In Dunn's book *Privatizing Poland* she describes a situation where an American company, having bought a Polish baby food enterprise, runs a campaign called: 'We See a Difference'. On a big board are pictured two identically looking carrots, both of which appear tasty and delicious. But only one of the carrots is certificated by the company, whereas the other could come from just any farm and potentially be dangerous for the child's health. The real concern of the company was that many Polish women tended to make their own baby food as this was perceived as essential to the role of being a caring mother (Dunn 2004). While Dunn analyzes this case as a means to create a new understanding of products I suggest that such campaigns likewise are aimed at changing an embedded sense of values and perceptions of motherhood among Polish women. Thereby they are creating, or making (to stay faithful to Dunn's vocabulary) a new customer.

[14] The function of Laisvės Aleja as a place for women to make an appearance dates back to Soviet times: after work, people would dress up in their best clothes, some of which had been obtained from Western Europe, and promenade up and down the street. At that time it was one of the only places to show (relative) material wealth.

Likewise is the creation of the new Lithuanian customer a prerequisite for success for standards and measurements. The problem remains for the EU, that just as Insiders may not, and Outsiders do not stay faithful to the standard regime, so do many customers operate with different ideas for what a good product really is. This became more interesting as new criteria were set and posed challenges to previous beliefs, stirred up the waters and impacted on ideas about products. Indeed, there was not (or no longer) a final consensus. The elevation of the national products in contrast to the food safety policy backed by the EU resulted in conflicting opinions in daily life. New understandings of hygiene would often conflict with perceptions of healthy milk straight from the cow. An agricultural advisor argued:

> The basic issue is that they [the Outsiders] do not have permission to sell [...] People buy from them because it is cheap. The problem is that [...] you never know what you get. There could be all kinds of bacteria. [...] That is why people need a special permission. And to get permission means that you have to go to many offices and milk institutes, you need a bunch of papers. The milk has to have the right temperature, do not get me started on the requirements for storage. And there should be no residual antibiotics in the milk. It is all very difficult. [...][15]

Whereas the advisor had imbedded his argumentation in the emerging discourse about food safety and hygiene, talking along the standard- and person-making lines, it was far from all those who had adapted to this way of thinking and instead found inconsistencies in the new regulations.[16] We can take the same logic to the market place: as long as the food products produced by the Outsiders are recognized as belonging to 'our' Lithuanian kitchen and being a part of the traditional food products, they may be excluded in space, but included in society. Furthermore, as long as customers recognize quality as linked with a well-known taste and production, EU warnings about food safety may have little impact on the customers' choice. To sum up: as long as the debate about authenticity and natural products straight from the cow are dominant among people who pursue the products, the Outsiders are still capable of gaining ground and negotiating a new position within (not outside) the EU framework for production. A customer, a man

---

[15] Interview, Kaunas municipal administration, November 2006.

[16] For a comparative discussion of the preferences in sausages, see Klumbyte, 2009.

in his early 50s, explained:

> I buy outside, and I always did. The reason some people buy inside is because they want to make sure what they get. [...] Let us say that I now go inside to buy. Then next weekend I go visit my mother in the countryside, and she gives me several litres of milk and a cheese to take home with me. Then I should say no to that too? What would the logic be in that? [...] I have eaten [these products] since I was a child. Meanwhile somebody in Brussels got this idea that my mum's milk is bad, because it has not been sent to a laboratory. [...] Then I should stay away from the milk I have been drinking for the past 50 years, because what used to make me healthy is now a danger to my health.[17]

As it is suggested in this quote, the logic behind the standard regime does not appeal to customers who perceive this food as real and nutritious Lithuanian produce, which, due to distant policy-making is all of a sudden embedded in a different category as low-quality. In order to be able to exclude illegal products from the market is it necessary to create a new kind of customer, or consumer, who internalizes the EUropeanized values. The problem emerges that just like the Polish mothers who operate with certain values of motherhood which are connected to their own production of baby food, so do the Lithuanians navigate in the market according to more nuanced internalized values about a healthy product, which likewise is connected with a sense of 'our' and 'home.'

Conclusion

In this article I have suggested that the links between standards and identity politics are moderated by socio-economic calculations by people subjected to the new standards regime, and by the re-evocation of the traditional products. Whereas the EU-control is pervasive, it is restricted to certain spaces, at certain times, for certain producers. The main reason why the standard policy appears so ineffective, I suggest, is because the EU project of 'making' people (producers and customers) does not work out in practice. The links between standards and the making of persons are influenced both by options and restrictions in the nearby environment, and also by the calculations and practical negotiations of the actors. Although

[17] From my field notes, January 2007.

Lithuania formally operates a zero-tolerance policy towards informal production of and sale of dairy products, this is on the practical level not perceived as a serious crime. Indeed, any given police officer could have been brought up on the same kind of cheese which now classified as illegal, and in most cases the police cannot be bothered to go to the market place, even when called up by angry Insiders. While justification through EU blueprinting appears only stimulating for the producers who, from the onset, have the knowledge and capabilities to become EUropean farmers, which is a minority, the EU unintentionally provided the Outsiders with a new frame of understanding for their production. They did not submit to the disqualification of the outside products but operated with a new frame for their milk and cheese products. They, in the midst of the growing importation of E-numbered products from the old member countries, reinvented the wheel. The authentic classic Lithuanian farm products now again appear 'traditional anew'. In such practical negotiations of both Insiders and Outsiders, and the failed person-making of both producers and customers, we find the weakness in the standard regime.

References

BARRY, Andrew
2001 *Governing a Technological Society*, London: Athlone Press.

BELLIER, Irène and Thomas M. WILSON
2000 'Building, Imagining, and Experiencing Europe: Institutions and Identities in the European Union.' Pp. 1-27 in Irène Bellier and Thomas M. Wilson (eds.), *An Anthropology of the European Union.* New York: Berg.

BENDA-BECKMANN, Franz von
1997 'Citizens, Strangers and Indigenous People: Conceptual Politics and Legal Pluralism.' *Law & Anthropology* 9: 1-43.

BENDA-BECKMANN, Franz von and Keebet von BENDA-BECKMANN
2006 'The Dynamics of Change and Continuity in Plural Legal Orders.' *Journal of Legal Pluralism* 53/53: 1-44.
2009 'Contested Spaces of Authority in Indonesia.' Pp. 115-135 in Franz von Benda-Beckmann, Keebet von Benda-Beckmann and Anne Griffiths (eds.), *Spatializing Law. An Anthropological Geography of Law in Society*. Farnham: Ashgate.

CALDWELL, Melissa
2009 'Introduction: Food and everyday life after socialism.' Pp. 1-28 in Melissa Caldwell (ed.), *Food and Everyday Life in the Postsocialist*

World. Bloomington: Indiana University Press.

DUNN, Elizabeth C.

2003 'Audit, Corruption and the Problem of Personhood: Scenes from Postsocialist Poland.' Pp. 127-146 in Wolf Lepenies (ed.), *Entangled Histories and Negotiated Universals. Centers and Peripheries in a Changing World*. Frankfurt, New York: Campus Verlag.

2004 *Privatizing Poland: Baby-food, Big Business and the Remaking of Labor*. Ithaca: Cornell University Press.

2005 'Standards and Person-Making in East Central Europe.' Pp. 173-193 in Aihwa Ong, and Stephen J. Collier (eds.), *Global Assemblages. Technology, Politics and Ethics as Anthropological Problems*. Malden, MA: Blackwell Publishing.

EHRLICH, Eugen

2002 *Fundamental Principles of the Sociology of Law* [first published in German 1913, in English 1936]. New Brunswick: Transaction Publishers.

GIDDENS, Anthony

2003 *Central Problems in Social Theory. Action, Structure and Contradiction in Social Analysis* [first published 1979]. Basingstoke: The Macmillan Press.

HARBOE KNUDSEN, Ida

2010 *Effects of Legal Changes in the Lithuanian Countryside after the Entrance to the EU*. PhD dissertation, Max Planck Institute for Social Anthropology, Halle/Saale, Germany.

HOHNEN, Pernille

2003 *A Market out of Place? Remaking Economic, Social and Symbolic Boundaries in Post-Communist Lithuania*. Oxford: Oxford University Press.

HUMPHREY, Caroline and Vera SKVIRSKAJA

2009 'Trading Places: Post-socialist container markets and the city.' *Focaal – European Journal of Anthropology* 55: 61-73.

KLUMBYTĖ, Neringa

2009 'The Geo-Politics of Taste, The "Euro" and Soviet Sausage Industries in Lithuania.' Pp. 130-153 in Melissa Caldwell (ed.), *Food and Everyday Life in the Postsocialist World*. Bloomington: Indiana University Press.

MINCYTE, Diana

2009 'Self-made Women: Informal Dairy Markets in Europeanizing Lithuania.' Pp. 78-100 in Melissa Caldwell (ed.), *Food and Everyday Life in the Postsocialist World*. Bloomington: Indiana University Press.

MOORE, Sally Falk

1978 *Law as Process: An Anthropological Approach*. Oxford: Oxford University Press for International African Institute.

MUNCK, Victor C. de
2008 'Millenarian Dreams: The Objects and Subjects of Money in the New Lithuania.' Pp. 171-191 in Ingo Schröder and Asta Vonderau (eds.,), *Changing Economies and Changing Identities in Post-Socialist Eastern Europe*. Münster: Lit-Verlag.

PINE, Frances
2001 'From Production to Consumption in Postsocialism?' Pp. 209-224 in Michal Buchowski (ed.), *Poland Beyond Communism. "Transition" in Critical Perspective*. Freiburg: Universitätsverlag.

ROBERTS, Simon
2007 'Order and the Evocation of Heritage: Representing Quality in the French Biscuit Trade.' Pp. 16-33 in Keebet von Benda-Beckmann and Fernanda Pirie (eds.), O*rder and Disorder. Anthropological Perspectives*. New York and Oxford: Berghahn Books.

SEWELL, William H. Jr.
1992 'A Theory of Structure: Duality, Agency, and Transformation.' *American Journal of Sociology* 98(1): 1-29.

SMIGIELSKA, Joanna
1992 'There's the Beef.' Pp. 110-121 in Janine R. Wedel (ed.), T*he Unplanned Society. Poland after Communism*. New York: Columbia University Press.

WALLACE, William V.
2000 'Enlarging the European Union, an Overview.' *Perspectives on European Politics and Society* 1(1): 1-18.

KHAT AND ISLAMIC LEGAL PERSPECTIVES: ISSUES FOR CONSIDERATION[1]

Heather Douglas and Abdi Hersi

Introduction

The leaves of the Khat (or Catha Edulis) plant are chewed for their stimulatory effect[2] by many people who live around the Red Sea, especially in Somalia, Djibouti and Yemen.[3] As people from countries where khat is commonly used have migrated throughout the world, they have brought with them the practice of chewing khat. This migration has required many countries to address the question of whether khat should be regulated, and if so, how. In Australia the debate about appropriate regulatory approaches to khat is just beginning (Douglas and Pedder, 2010). In contrast, in countries such as the United Kingdom and Canada the question of how to regulate khat has been a contested issue for some time (Sykes et

[1] This research was supported by a grant from the National Drug Law Enforcement Research Fund.

[2] The khat plant contains several active constituents, including cathinone and cathine. Cathinone is the most potent constituent contained in the plant and possesses a chemical structure very similar to amphetamine. Cathinone is responsible for much of the stimulant effect of khat. The young leaves and leaf tips, which are preferred for chewing, are understood to contain higher proportions of cathinone (Graziani, Milella and Nencini 2008: 762).

[3] Khat is also chewed in Eastern African countries including Rwanda, Tanzania, Uganda, Kenya and Madagascar (WHO 2006).

al 2010; Klein and Metaal 2010: 586). To date studies of khat have tended to focus on the health effects of chewing the plant on individuals (Elmi 1983; Al-Hebshi and Skaug 2005; Gebissa 2004; Armstrong, 2008) and the economic effects on communities that consume, trade and cultivate the plant (Tefera 2009). While impacts on health and the economy are clearly important considerations in determining appropriate legal regulation, we argue here that because khat use is mainly associated with Muslim people (Armstrong 2008: 632), the Islamic law about khat is also an important consideration in this debate. The question of whether the use of khat is lawful pursuant to Islamic shari'a has attracted little attention from academics, researchers and policy makers. With the exception of several internet blogs (eg. Sunni Forum 2010) and Islamic websites (e.g. University Sains Islam Malaysia 2010) that provide a decree about the legality of khat according to Islamic shari'a, there is little exploration of the use of khat from the perspective of Islam. In response to this perceived gap in the literature this article explores the position of khat pursuant to Islamic law. Relevant passages from the Qu'ran and prophetical traditions are considered along with other sources of Islamic shari'a. In 2010 we conducted focus groups with Somali people who had settled in Australia and a number of participants commented directly on the relationship between their understanding of the Islamic position on khat and their decision to chew the plant. In many cases it was participants' interpretation of unofficial, or Islamic law, rather than State law that guided their decision to chew khat. The participants' views are also considered in this discussion.

We argue that an appreciation of the debates taking place between Islamic scholars, and within those communities that use khat, is important in the development of regulatory frameworks regarding khat in Australia and other Western states where khat regulation is controversial. This article begins with a general consideration of the role of Islam in regulating khat in Common Law countries such as Australia before setting out the methodological approach in relation to the focus group data collected. The article then goes on to explore the three main Islamic legal positions that have been claimed in relation to khat. We conclude with some suggestions for the way forward.

Regulating khat

Although Australia is generally considered to be a secular state (Hudson 2003: 425) the consideration of religion can and should make an important contribution to public debate (Audi 1989: 278-279). Indeed there may be risks in excluding religious considerations from such discussions. In particular Maddox (2006: 309) suggests that excluding religion from debate may strengthen its power or result in alienation fostering extremism (see also Davies 2009: 76). Hudson suggests that Australian citizenship has 'religious features' and that multicultural countries like Australia should consider themselves multi-faith rather than secular (2003: 429). In a sense the Australian Constitution reflects this position when it exhorts that "the Commonwealth may not make any law ... for prohibiting the free exercise of any religion ..." (Australian Constitution 1900: section 116). If we consider Australia as multi-faith, this view has implications for the consideration of legal issues (Hudson 2003: 429). In the context of regulating khat, particular considerations may include whether khat should be prohibited, and culpability and sentencing questions (Douglas and Pedder 2010: 300). Religion generally, and Islam specifically, is arguably a feature of Australian citizenship. In Australia 74 percent of people report a religious affiliation and approximately two percent of the population identify as Muslim and this number is steadily increasing (ABS 2004).

Islam may be described as a system of law that co-exists with state law in common law countries; generally it is considered to be a form of unofficial law (Griffiths 1986). Drawing on Davies' discussion of legal pluralism we can say that Islamic law presents an 'alternative sphere of normative ordering' that 'exists alongside legal regulation' (2008: 287; see also Moore 1973). Many scholars accept that the power of law is not limited to a single site; rather it is located in multiple sites and may include alternative practices of law (Davies 2008: 286). In the Australian context, it has been argued that legal pluralism is already a reality and that shari'a operates as a form of unofficial law and non-state legal ordering (Black 2008: 214). Scholars of Islam, and those who follow Islam, disagree as to the extent to which shari'a must be followed in non-Muslim countries (Abou El Fadl 1994: 151-153). As a result, in Australia, and other common law countries where khat chewing is predominantly associated with Muslim communities, Islamic law may provide an authoritative statement governing a person's decision to chew, despite existing state law (Klein 2008: 830).

In Christian communities the view of khat is not absolutely consistent. Khat is tolerated in certain circles of African Christian communities while in others it is perceived to be an ungodly and unholy plant. For example, in Kenya, Meru people who are Christian, are known to chew khat (Anderson and Carrier 2009) while some Ethiopian Christian Orthodox communities have referred to the plant as cursed, "relating that when God came to Earth all the plants bowed before him - showing their ultimate reverence. The exception was khat: a plant which stood straight with a posture of disrespect. Then God cursed - *forever you be chewed by humans*" (Anderson et al 2007: 2). In East African nations where Christianity is the principal religion, for example Kenya and Uganda, the consumption of Khat is anecdotally believed to be higher in the provinces and regions where Muslims are a majority of the population. While some Yemeni Jews and Ethiopian Christians use Khat (Gebissa 2008: 83), the practice in Yemen and Ethiopia is generally associated with Muslims (Varisco 1986: 3). Gebissa reports that in Ethiopian orthodox Christian communities, khat chewing is seen to be a sign of conversion to the Muslim faith (Gebissa 2004: 52). In Ethiopia, the proportion of Christians and Muslims is fairly even, and in 2009 it was reported that it was mainly Muslim people who used khat in that country (Lamina and Babu 2009: 53). The association between Muslims and khat consumption is also emphasised by Anderson and others who observe that khat has played a symbolic function to distinguish Christianity from Islamic powers (Anderson et al 2007: 2).

Thus there is a strong association between Muslims and the consumption of khat and it is reported that Muslims are the major consumers of khat worldwide (Armstong 2008: 632). Predominantly Muslim nations such as Yemen, Somalia, and Djibouti are identified as nations where the consumption of Khat is particularly prevalent (Armstrong 2008). In these countries over 90 percent of the population identifies as Muslim (Pew Forum on Religion and Public Life 2010). Similarly in the diaspora communities of immigrants from East African and Horn of Africa communities in Australia, the United Kingdom, Canada and the United States, khat chewing is associated with Muslim people (Stevenson et al 1996: 75-77). In Australia khat chewing has been strongly associated with the Somali community most of whom are Muslim (Fitzgerald and Lawrence 2009: 4).

There is an increasing Muslim migrant population from the countries of the East African and Horn of Africa regions to common law countries including Australia, Canada, the United Kingdom and the United States (United States Department of Homeland Security 2009: 14; Australian Bureau of Statistics 2004). Some suggest that khat utilisation is central to the lives of many members of these immigrant communities including those in the United States (Armstrong 2008: 631). However, there are uncertainties about the Islamic legal perspective on khat and its significance to the increasing number of new immigrants to Australia (Fitzgerald and Lawrence 2009: 10). In order to consider the role of Islam in the Somali diaspora community in Australia we undertook a number of focus groups. The methodology we used in our study is discussed in the next section of this article.

Methodology

Over the course of 2010 the researchers carried out nineteen focus groups with men and women of Somali background in four Australian states: Queensland, New South Wales, Western Australia and Victoria. A key advantage of focus groups is that participants are encouraged to discuss their ideas and responses to problems and the researcher can facilitate and hear these discussions. Morgan observes that it is important that participants feel safe in expressing opinions and this will usually mean setting up a relatively homogenous group (Morgan 1998: 81, 91). There will sometimes be disagreement and participants need to feel comfortable when expressing different opinions. Thus in establishing a focus group to discuss views on controversial topics (such as khat), participants may be more comfortable expressing their views if they know the other members of the group share a particular outlook. The venue is also an important consideration, as it can have an impact on recruitment and the comfort of participants. While homogeneity of participants may help to provide a safe environment for sharing views, there are limitations implicit in this approach as well. Necessarily, responses are likely to compound certain views of the particular group. This underlines the need to carry out a number of focus groups with different types of groups to ensure a breadth of views.

Participants for this study were recruited with the assistance of relevant community cultural associations. 114 people took part in the focus groups. The mean number of participants in the focus groups was 8 participants. 89 participants were men and 35 were women. Separate groups were conducted according to two factors: gender and whether participants identified as users or non-users of khat. Despite these distinctions on some occasions 'non-users' stated in the focus groups that they did actually use khat sometimes. Interpreters in Somali were present and focus group discussions were recorded and transcribed. Themes were later extracted from the transcripts. Both interpreters and facilitators were the same gender as members of the focus group. For our research we conducted focus groups in the meeting areas used by the cultural organisations that assisted in the recruitment process and in local community meeting rooms. Most participants in the focus groups would have previously visited the spaces used so it was generally a familiar environment. A number of the participants discussed the relationship between Islam and khat. It should be noted that in New South Wales and Victoria khat use and possession is not prohibited while in Queensland and Western Australia it is illegal to possess khat (Douglas and Pedder 2010). Regardless of these differences in State law, the participants in our focus groups held divergent views on the Islamic position on khat and many participants referred to Islamic law rather than State law to explain why it was acceptable or unacceptable to chew the plant. The study participants' views are discussed in the following section of this article along with competing scholarly views of the Islamic position on khat.

Islam and Khat

The spirituality and status of khat varies both between Muslim groups and between individual Muslims in East Africa and the Arabian Peninsula (Rahman 1979: 223). The geographical region, culture and the sect of Islam all play a role in how individuals and groups of Muslim people perceive khat; thus because Islam "operates in distinctive ways in local contexts, there is a range of Islams" (Black 2008: 217; Al-Azmeh 1996). For example in Yemen and Uganda, where the practice of shari'a is applied mainly to matters such as marriage, divorce, inheritance, and civil issues, religious opinion generally sanctions the use of Khat (Varisco 1986: 1). In contrast, Saudi Arabia, a sovereign Arab Islamic state where a more fundamentalist Islam is practised, outlawed khat decades ago (Beckerleg 2008: 752). In Somalia the position has fluctuated regularly. There are a number of controversies and uncertainties about khat's health and financial impacts (Odenwald et al 2010) and controversies and uncertainties extend to Islamic legal rulings about the plant (Lamina 2010: 3). A community engagement forum conducted in the United Kingdom by the National Drugs and Race Equality Forum found that depending on which sheikh's teachings are followed, members of the United Kingdom Somali community may view khat use as harmless and halal (permissible) or haram (impermissible) (Buffin et al 2008: 6). Inconsistency arises in part as a result of the interpretation of the key sources of Islamic law that are used to identify guiding principles. These are, first, the Qur'an, followed by prophetical traditions known as the Sunna and Hadith (sayings and practices of the prophet Muhammed (pbuh)) then Ijma (the consensus of scholars) and Qiyas (the process of deductive analogy) (Rahman 1979; Movsesian 2010: 867). These four sources of Islamic law are accepted by Muslim scholars (Michalak and Trocki 2006: 527-534). According to Muslims, the Qur'an is the final revelation of God to humankind and Ulema (Islamic scholars) unanimously agree that it is the most authoritative guide for Muslims and the first source of the shari'a (Movsesian 2010: 867).

Across the Muslim world, opinion is sharply divided amongst Islamic scholars and Muftis on the correct approach to khat. The three main positions on khat are that it is halal (permissible), makruh (detested or discouraged) or haram (forbidden). The debate between sections of the Islamic community in regard to the permissibility and impermissibility of khat is based on the inferences made in various verses in the Qu'ran and some prophetical traditions known as Hadith where they relate to intoxicants. The key to these debates lies in how the intoxicating elements that are found in the shrub khat and their impact on the human body and society at large are understood.

A well known Muslim scholar, Shatibi, argues that a balance must be struck between adherence to the texts' apparent meaning and the law giver's intention (Al Raysuni 2006: 46). It must be emphasised that the current debates on the legality of khat in the Islamic law are inherently part of the broader debate about whether or not Islamic shari'a is rigid or flexible and how far it is able to address changing social circumstances (Rahman 1979). The three main Islamic perspectives on khat are explored below. The debates about the religiosity and spirituality of Khat consumption are not constrained to the past. Many individuals within the Somali Muslim communities we spoke to used religious texts to confirm the permissibility or impermissibility of khat use in contemporary society and examples of their comments are included in the discussion below.

The *Halal* (Lawful/Legal) Discourse on Khat

Some argue that the deep rooted Islamic religious and cultural traditions associated with khat consumption have persisted from the fifteenth and sixteenth centuries (Anderson et al 2007: 3). Tradition was referred to by a number of the participants in our study as a justification for the halal position of khat. For example a Victorian Somali woman in our study observed: 'it has been used generation by generation ... It's been used in the Qu'ran; it's been used in religious occasions.' While in response to the question: 'Why can't you live without khat?', a Victorian Somali man commented: 'because it is our tradition, it is our way of life, we grow up with it - we enjoy it a lot. It doesn't harm us, it doesn't harm anyone.'

In the literature the khat plant has been referred to by a number of spiritual and religious terms including the 'elixir of life', 'the flower of paradise' (Anderson et al 2007: 2; Varisco 1986: 1) and 'qut ul salihin' which translates from Arabic as 'sustenance of the righteous' (Wagner 2005: 125). A well-known writer on khat, Gebissa, recounts the following words of an interviewee in one of his studies:

> Khat is a tree that God loves. It's a tree blessed by Rabi (God)

> and given to us. This is a tree that man cannot command. A lot of people with power have tried to control it, especially the price of selling the leaves. None has succeeded so far. This tree is not just another ordinary plant; it is a 'Leaf of Allah'. (Gebissa (2004: 3)

Khat's existence and discovery has been linked to mysticism by some writers. For example Wagner refers to a story attributed to Yemeni people wherein the legendary prophet, Dhul Qarnayn, brought khat to Ethiopia from China in order to rid the country of pestilence and jinn (Wagner 2005: 123).[4] Proponents of the halal argument claim that there are a number of spiritual rituals that are aided by the consumption of khat including reading the Qur'an and performing prayers. For example one study conducted in Ethiopia showed that 80 percent of chewers used khat to gain a good level of concentration for prayers and to facilitate contact with God (Varisco 1986: 3). Similarly, members of the Sufi sect of Islam have sometimes approved the consumption of khat for gaining concentration in relation to religious practices (Gebissa 2004: 7; Armstrong 2008: 632). A Victorian woman in our study observed: "We are 100 per cent Muslim. Yes we do Qu'ran sometimes while we eat it. We'll listen to Qu'ran you know while we chew khat but we listen to music too. So we've got both." Similarly a Western Australian man observed: "Some people use khat to get closer, to get more energy for their worship". It is claimed that khat is also an accepted part of other Muslim religious activities. For example, it has been suggested that chewing khat is a central activity during the week long Yemeni wedding celebrations (Wagner 2005: 137). Once the premise is accepted, that khat is religiously significant, it is argued by some that the continuation of Khat consumption in common law countries by Muslim immigrant groups should be tolerated as part of a commitment to multiculturalism (Armstrong 2008: 632).

Proponents of the halal position also rely on the fact that there is not a verse in the Qu'ran that explicitly mentions khat or its prohibition. It is claimed by some that the lack of specific reference to khat in the Qu'ran or the Sunna, the two most authoritative principal guides of Islamic shari'a, means that khat must be halal (Omar and Besseling 2008: 3). A male interviewee based in Queensland stated:

> I don't find that [khat is not permitted] in the Qu'ran. I don't find

[4] Jinn are one of the three creations of Allah, like humans they have free will but less strength of will than humans (Mohammed 2004: 30).

> that the Sunna has got anything to say about that... that is two things that we have to look into. To make something illegal in Islam... you either have to have it in the Hadith, or in the Sunna.

Khat is understood by many Muslims to be permissible pursuant to the Qur'an as an alternative to alcohol. While scholars generally agree that the Qur'an expressly prohibits alcohol use (Michalak and Trocki 2006: 529) no such clear prohibition exists for khat. In the Qur'an drinking alcohol, and drinking wine specifically, is identified as a disruptive social evil. One verse states:

> And from the fruits of date-palms and grapes, you derive strong drink [this was before the order of the prohibition of the alcoholic drinks] and a goodly provision. Verily, therein is indeed a sign for people who have wisdom (Qur'an 16:67; Michalek and Trioci 2006: 528).

Islam has gradually implemented a four step prohibition approach to alcohol (Michalak and Trocki 2006: 527-534) and consequently, there are few disagreements about the rulings on alcohol in the Qur'an. Many of the focus group participants in our study contrasted alcohol specifically with khat. For example women in Victoria made the following comments: "It's not alcohol. It's not hashish. It's something that makes you calm and we eat with tea", and:

> Facilitator: Do you drink alcohol...?
> Speaker 1: No. It's against religion.
> Facilitator: But khat is okay?
> Speaker 2: Khat is ours.

Some of the participants specifically claimed that while alcohol is intoxicating, khat is not. For example Victorian women commented:

> So drinking alcohol of course changes the whole mentality, you know the whole of thinking. You know you lose control. When you're walking ... balance is losing so that is where it's looked at, but Khat doesn't do that. So that's where it's safe... it's not a drug.
>
> Does Khat affect someone? No. Does alcohol affect someone? Yes, because we know what they do [under the influence of

> alcohol] and they say words that they didn't want to say and they regret later on when the alcohol gets out of the body.

The question of whether khat is recognised as an 'intoxicant' by Islamic scholars is contested and is discussed further below in the section of this article relating to the haram position.

The *Makruh* (Detested/Discouraged) Discourse on Khat.

The claim that khat is detested and discouraged or 'makruh' reflects a risk-averse middle ground. Makruh is explained to be something which is not bad if it is consumed in moderation, but if used in excess becomes haram (Movsesian 2010: 870). Beckerleg notes that the former chief Mufti of Uganda is one of the pioneering growers of Khat and believes that khat is neither halal nor haram (Beckerleg 2006: 229). The Makruh argument with respect to khat considers khat in a similar way to tobacco smoking. Generally tobacco smoking is tolerated because of its perceived mild effect (Ghouri et al 2006: 265). Some of the participants in our study made comments that imply support for the makruh position suggesting that as long as one did not overuse khat, chewing khat is halal. Only when khat is overused or the person becomes addicted to khat does use of the plant become haram. For example two men in Queensland had the following conversation:

> Speaker 1: ...if we look for addicts khat can be haram in certain jurisdictions. If you – everything you use over can affect you mentally...
> Speaker 2: And if it gets overused.
> Speaker 1: Yes overused has been a negative effect... Only if you expend over your [budget] for your family - so this is a habit... according to Islamic religion if you use it more than – and it affects your mental disorder then it becomes haram.

Other participants claimed that there was a relaxed position that supported individual approaches to the plant. For example another man in Queensland suggested: "some might have religious matters". Another male participant from Western Australia claimed that until there was clearer information about the impacts and effects of khat its Islamic legal status was unclear: "the main problem is the people ...don't have evidence of any [disease], or any other effects, so no one can exactly straight away say this is haram, full stop". Arguably, the Makruh position is the weakest position and is probably adopted by a minority group of scholars. Some scholars argue that the Makruh position may contradict a prophetical tradition (or Hadith) that states that: 'what intoxicates in large amounts is prohibited even if taken in small amounts' (Michalak and Trocki 2006: 529). This is discussed further below.

The *Haram* (Prohibition) Discourse on Khat

The position that presumes khat is prohibited or haram is supported by a number of scholars of Islam. Two related arguments are relevant here. The first is that khat should be defined as an intoxicant and once it is defined in this way it must be considered haram. The second argument relies on the claim that khat should be considered haram in order to preserve human interests. In this second chain of argument it is argued that the negative effects of khat exceed its benefits and it is thus haram. These two arguments are discussed in turn below.

The term 'khamr' is used in the Qu'ran and is often translated to mean 'wine' in Arabic, however the word is understood generally to have the broader meaning of 'intoxicant' (Michalak and Trocki 2006: 528). There are a number of accepted Hadith that relate to intoxicants and they may also cover khat if khat is understood to be an intoxicant. Michalak and Trocki refer to a number of examples of relevant Hadith in this context such as: 'every intoxicant is khamr and every khamr is haram' (Michalak and Trocki 2006: 529). Thus if khat is considered to be an intoxicant it is, inevitably, haram, regardless of how much is used. A Queensland man in our study commented: "There is an Islamic formula ...which means if you eat a large amount of something and [it] intoxicates you, eating small amounts of it still falls into the category of haram which means unlawful category".

Some Ulemas (Muslim scholars trained in Islamic law) apply a broad definition to the word khamr and rely on a series of prophetical traditions that focus on the necessary human interest and the concepts of 'Maqasid' or higher objectives of Islamic shari'a. These scholars reject the reliance on the text of the Qur'an and Hadith as the only sources of Islamic law. Instead, they use a mixture of sources of Islamic law to advance their case. For instance, some argue that the Qur'an is supplemented by Sunna (or practices of the prophet), but the meaning of the Sunna is determined by the Qur'an (Masud 1995: 247). The rationale is that Islamic law clearly stipulates that whatever clouds the mind is khamr and therefore should be regarded as harmful. In support of this position some point to various verses in the Qu'ran. For example one particular verse states that one must not perform prayers while one is intoxicated (Qur'an 4:43).

There are a number of Hadiths that are understood to supplement the Qur'anic verses about intoxicants. For example Abi Burda narrates the following:

> That Abu Musa Al-Ash'ari said that the Prophet had sent him to Yemen and he asked the Prophet about certain (alcoholic) drink which used to be prepared there The Prophet said, "What are they?" Abu Musa said, "Al-Bit' and Al-Mizr?" He said, "Al-Bit is an alcoholic drink made from honey; and Al-Mizr is an alcoholic drink made from barley." The Prophet said, "All intoxicants are prohibited." (*Translation of Sahih Bukhari*, Book 59: *Volume 5; Book 59: Number 631, available at Centre for Muslim Jewish Engagement 2011)*

In the Islamic jurisprudence known as Fiqh, there are four major *Madhabs,* or schools of thought, in classical Sunni Islam emanating from four Imams (Movsesian 2010: 861, 870). When these four Imams were writing, Khat was not a known substance. However, these Imams discuss hashish and nutmeg and subsequently some scholars equate khat to hashish and nutmeg because of its effect on its users. Sheikh Mohamed Ibn Ibrahim has reported that all the four major Islamic schools of thought – Shafi'e, Maliki, Ahmady literally and Hanbali by deduction, agree that Nutmeg is haram (PCSR 2011). From this, his thesis argues that it is the general meaning of 'khamr' that is the key and consequently khat may be deemed to be unlawful. Accordingly, Sheikh Mohamed Ibn Ibrahim reports that unlawfulness of khat applies to its consumption and further to cultivation and supply (PCSR 2011).

The question is whether khat is defined as an intoxicant. The effects of alcohol and khat are quite different: alcohol is a depressant while the effects of khat are stimulatory. Some of the participants in our study questioned whether khat is indeed 'intoxicating', but overwhelmingly study participants also accepted that khat caused them to become 'stimulated,' 'more awake and energetic' and 'more sociable'. These experiences are consistent with pharmacological studies about the effects of khat (Graziani et al 2008: 762). A male participant from Queensland commented:

> ...because we are mostly people from the Somali community. And there is a significant number of Somali community who are ... eating or chewing the khat or also selling or buying. ...even though we are duty bound to abide by the laws of Queensland, in general the laws of Australia, but Islamically khat is not lawful because it is classified... as an intoxicant. And whatever is toxic according to the Islamic verdict it is unlawful. Therefore it should be illegal in the first place.

A male participant in Western Australia claimed that khat is addictive and observed: "It's addictive, like a drug. Drug is haram." A noted scholar on Islam, Kasule, suggests that 'intoxicants change or impair the intellect or the mind' and for that reason alone are impermissible (Kasule 2007). Clearly khat does affect the way a person responds to their surroundings and to this extent could be considered to be an intoxicant.

Some Islamic jurists and scholars have also used the concept of the 'Preservation of Necessary Human Interest' to argue that khat is haram. The necessary human interests to be preserved are determined by Muslim scholars to be the following five matters in order of importance: protection of faith, life, lineage, intellect and property (Kamali 2006: 16). Accordingly the test is that if it is the case that khat has a negative effect on any of the five necessary human interests, it then becomes haram.

Consistent with the 'Preservation of Necessary Human Interest' argument Maqasid *Al Sharia*, or the higher objectives of Islamic law, are also used to argue that Khat is forbidden. By using the concept of public interest *(Masalih Al Mursalah),* some Ulema have explored the plant's effects on health, economy and society and on the environment. For example khat crops in Yemen are negatively effecting the environment, society and the economy through the depletion of scarce water resources as a result of irrigation (Al-Mugahed 2009: 742). Similarly in Somalia khat use is recognised as a drain on the economy (Poore 2009: 135). Thus it is claimed that it is the preservation of the greater good of mankind that supports the impermissibility of khat. Social and economic effects of khat have been discussed in a number of studies (eg Sykes et al 2010) and they were also identified by a number of the participants in our study. For example a Queensland man commented that the high expenditure on khat by some users negatively affected families. He commented: "Also in the Koran ... Allah doesn't like those who are extravagant who spend their wealth unwisely. In those categories I am very confident to say that khat is haram which means unlawful in the first place." Similarly a New South Wales woman observed:

> You could also be addicted to it, some people use less maybe on the weekend just to socialise. Some people, they can't control. Every night they buy it and use it so that means that all their income goes to khat instead of supporting their family. Or maybe even get more money out the family instead of saving for them. It's like a drug I think.

A Western Australian man accepted that Muslim scholars were divided but he observed that some scholars claim that:

> ...the mere fact of someone sitting for eight continuous hours and wasting the time which God almighty has given to him. Based on that alone, [scholars] will say that wasting that time on something which is not beneficial is totally un-Islamic and unlawful.

There are a number of examples of prohibition of khat by Islam in African nations. For example, most Salafi scholars in the Arabian Peninsula and other places such as Somalia consider khat use to be haram. In Saudi Arabia, the Permanent Committee for Scholarly Research and Ifta (PCSR) which comprises a group of eminent Muslim scholars has banned the leaves and buds of stimulants like khat (PCSR 2008). Similarly, the hardline Islamic Courts Union in Somalia prohibited the consumption of Khat immediately after they gained control of most of the southern part of Somalia. Furthermore, it is reported that "most conservative elements in Kenya's Muslim community argue that Mira [a type of khat] is forbidden" (Carrier 2008: 811).

Conclusions

While the Islamic position on khat is far from clear, most of those who participated in our focus groups had a strong view on the correct position pursuant to Islam and this view influenced their decision to support or reject prohibition and to chew or not to chew khat. This supports the claim that legal pluralism is a reality in Australia (Black 2008). For many Somali people living in Australia there are two laws that have influence in their lives. While the Islamic legal perspectives on khat discussed here are not consistent, they add an important dimension to the general debates about the stimulant leaf and should not be ignored. In countries like Australia that purport to allow the free exercise of religion, prohibition of khat use may have implications to this freedom for some individuals. If khat is seen by some Muslims as an accepted part of cultural life and Muslim religious activity, targeting khat may then be seen as targeting these communities (Armstrong 2008: 641). In those states where khat is already prohibited a consideration of the background and motivation of those charged with khat related offences may be important to an understanding of culpability and in deciding on an appropriate sentence (Renteln and Valladares 2009: 201). Given that the overwhelming majority of khat users in Australia, and other common law states, are Muslim immigrants, the uncertain status of khat in Islam poses significant challenges to policy makers in immigrant receiving nations. As these communities' cultural norms are, to a large extent, derived from the Islamic religion, any government response to the use of khat should take into consideration these religious and cultural norms. As observed earlier, there are potential risks for government authorities if they are perceived to be making a ruling on a deeply held religious matter.

References

ABOU EL FADL, Khaled
1994 'Legal Debates on Muslim Minorities: Between Rejection and Accommodation.' *Journal of of Religious Ethics* 22: 127-162.

ABS (AUSTRALIAN BUREAU OF STATISTICS)
2004 'Religious Affiliation and Activity.' Paper 4.102.0 *Australian Social Trends*, http://www.abs.gov.au/Ausstats/abs@.nsf/1020492cfcd63696ca2568a1002477b5/fa58e975c470b73cca256e9e00296645!OpenDocument (viewed 7 January 2011).

AL-AZMEH, Aziz
1996 *Islams and Modernities*. London: Verso.

AL-HEBSHI, N. N., and N SKAUG
2005 'Khat (Catha Edulis) - An Updated Review.' *Addiction Biology* 10: 299-307.

AL-MUGAHED, Leen
2008 'Khat Chewing in Yemen: Turning Over a New Leaf.' *Bulletin of the World Health Organisation* 86(10): 741-742.

AL RAYSUNI, Amad
2006 *Imam al-Shatibi's theory of higher objectives and intents of Islamic law.* Kuala Lumpur: Islamic Book Trust
ANDERSON, David, and Neil CARRIER
2009 'Khat in Colonial Kenya: A History of Prohibition and Control.' *Journal of African History* 50: 377-397,
ANDERSON, David, Susan BECKERLEG, Degol HAILU and Axel KLEIN
2007 *The Khat Controversy: Stimulating the Debate on Drugs*. New York: Berg Publishers.
ARMSTRONG, Edward
2008 'Research Note. Crime, Chemicals and Culture: On the Complexity of Khat.' *Journal of Drug Issues* 38(2): 631-648.
AUSTRALIAN CONSTITUTION
1900 Commonwealth of Australia Constitution Act. Available at: http://www.aph.gov.au/senate/general/constitution/index.htm (accessed 2 February 2011).
BECKERLEG, Susan
2006 'What Harm? Kenyans and Ugandan Perspectives on Khat.' *African Affairs* 105(419): 219-241.
BLACK, Ann
2008 'Accommodating Shariah Law in Australia's legal System: Can we? Should we?' *Alternative Law Journal* 33(4): 214-219.
BUFFIN, Jez, Yaser MIR and Imran MIRZA
2009 'Khat: current views from the community around the UK – findings from Community engagement forums.' London: National Drugs and Race Equality Coalition.
CARRIER, Neil
2008 'Is Mira a Drug?: Categorizing Kenyan Khat.' *Substance Use and Misuse* 43: 803-818.
CENTRE FOR MUSLIM-JEWISH ENGAGEMENT
2011 'Compendium of Muslim Texts.' University of Southern Carolina, http://www.usc.edu/schools/college/crcc/engagement/resources/texts/muslim/search.html (accessed 7 February 2011).
DAVIES, Margaret
2008 'Feminism and the Flat Law Theory.' *Feminist Legal Studies* 16: 281-304.
2009 'Pluralism in law and religion.' Pp72-99 in Peter Cane, Carolyn Evans and Zoe Robinson (eds.), *Law and Religion in Theoretical and Historical Context*. Cambridge: Cambridge University Press.

DOUGLAS, Heather, and Merali PEDDER
2010 'Legal Regulation of the drug khat in Australia.' *Journal of Law and Medicine* 18(2): 284-301.
ELMI, Abdullahi S.
1983 'The Chewing of Khat in Somalia.' *Journal of Ethnopharmacology,* 8: 163-176.
FITZGERALD, John, and Louise LAWRENCE
2009 *Khat: A Literature Review.* Melbourne: Centre for Culture, Ethnicity and Health.
GEBISSA, Ezekiel
2004 *Leaf of Allah: Khat and Agricultural Transformation in Harerge, Ethiopia 1875-1991.* Oxford: James Currey Ltd.
2008 'Scourge of Life or an Economic Lifeline? Public Discourses on Khat (*Catha edulis*) in Ethiopia.' *Substance Use and Misuse* 43(6): 784-802.
GHOURI, Nazim, Mohammed ATCHA and Aziz SHEIKH
2006 'Public health: Influence of Islam on smoking among Muslims.' *British Medical Journal* 332: 291-294.
GRAZIANI, Manuela, Michele S. MILELLA and Paolo NENCINI
2008 'Khat Chewing from the Pharmacological Point of View: An Update.' *Substance Use and Misuse* 43: 762 –783.
GRIFFITHS, John
1986 'What is legal pluralism?' *Journal of Legal Pluralism* 24: 1-55.
HUDSON, Wayne
2003 'The Chewing of Khat in Somalia.' *Australian Journal of Politics and History* 49: 425-429.
KAMALI, Mohammad
2006 *An Introduction to Shariah.* Kuala Lumpur: Ilmiah.
KASULI, Omar Hasan
2007 'Protection, Preservation, and Promotion of the Intellect, Hifdh Al Aql.' Paper presented at Symposium on Protection of the Aql, Kulliyah of Medicine, International Islamic University Kuantan available at: http://omarkasule-04.tripod.com/id1290.html (accessed 7 February 2011).
KLEIN, Axel
2008 'Khat in the Neighbourhood - Local Government Responses to Khat Use in a London Community.' *Substance Use and Misuse* 43: 819 -831.
KLEIN, Axel and Pien METAAL
2010 'A good chew or good riddance—How to move forward in the regulation of khat consumption.' *Journal of Ethnopharmacology* 132(3): 584-589.
MADDOX, Marion
2006 *God Under Howard: The Rise of the Religious Right in Australian*

Politics. Crows Nest: Allen & Unwin.

MASUD, Muhammed

1995 *Shatibi's Philosophy of Islamic Law*. Kula Lumpur: Islamic Book Trust.

MICHALAK, Laurence, and Karen TROCKI

2006 'Alcohol and Islam: An Overview.' *Contemporary Drug Problems* 33: 523-562.

MOHAMMED, Khaleel

2004 'A Muslim Perspective on Human Rights.' *Humanities Social Sciences and the Law* 41(2): 29-35.

MOORE, Sally Falk

1973 'Law and Social Change: The Semi-Autonomous Social Field as an Approriate Subject of Study.' *Law and Society Review* 7: 719-746.

MORGAN, David L.

1998 *The Focus Group Guidebook,* Thousand Oaks: Sage.

MOVSESIAN, Mark

2010 'Religious Legal Theory: The State of the Field.' *Seton Hall Law Review* 40: 861-889.

ODENWALD, Michael, Axel KLEIN and Nasir WARFA

2010 'Introduction to the Special Issue: The changing use and misuse of khat (Catha edulis) – Tradition, trade and tragedy.' *Journal of Ethnopharmacology* 132: 537-539.

OMAR, Ashar, and Renee BESSELING

2008 *Khat: A Drug of Growing Abuse*. Sweden: Bloms Trycker AB.

POORE, Brad

2009 'Somaliland: Shackled to a Failed State.' *Stanford Law Review* 45: 117-150.

RAHMAN, Fazlur

1979 'Towards Reformulating the methodology of Islamic Law: Sheikh Yamani on "Public Interest" in Islamic Law.' *Journal of International Law and Politics* 219: 219-224.

LAMINA, Sikiru

2010 'Khat (*Catha edulis*): The Herb with Officio-Legal, Socio-Cultural and Economic Uncertainty.' *South African Journal of Science* 106 (3/4): 1-4.

LAMINA, Sikiru, and Subramanian M. BABU

2009 'Khat (*Catha edulis*): Academic, Health and Psychological Effects on "mature" Students.' *African Journal of Drug & Alcohol Studies*. 8(2), 49-59.

PCSR (Permanent Committee for Scholarly Research and Ifta)

2008 *Permanent Committee Fatwas Kingdom of Saudi Arabia*, Group 1,

Volume 22, Fatwa 2159.

PEW FORUM ON RELIGION AND PUBLIC LIFE
2009 *Mapping the Global Muslim Population*. Washington: The Pew Forum on Religion and Public Life.

RENTELN, Alison Dundes, and Rene VALLADARES,
2009 'The Importance of Culture for the Justice System.' *Judicature* 92(5): 194-201.

STEWART, David W., Prem N. SHANDASANI and Dennis W. ROOK
2007 *Focus groups: Theory and practice'* 2nd ed. Thousand Oaks: Sage.

STEVENSON Mark, John FITZGERALD and Cathy BANWELL
1996 'Chewing as a Social Act: Cultural Displacement and Khat Consumption in the East African Communities of Melbourne.' *Drug and Alcohol Review* 15: 73-82.

SUNNI FORUM
2010 'Hard to Find Fatwa (khat)' available at: <http://www.sunniforum.com/forum/showthread.php?33366-Hard-to-Find-Fatwa-(khat)> (visited 30 November 2010)

TEFERA, Tesfaye Lemma
2009 'Supply response, local reality and livelihood sustainability: The Policy Dilemma of Khat (*Catha Edulis*) Production in Eastern Ethiopia.' *International Journal of Agricultural Sustainability* 7(3): 176-188.

SYKES, Wendy, Nick COLEMAN, Philly DESAI, Carola GROOM, Mohamed GURE and Radhika HOWARTH
2010 *Perceptions of the Social Harms Associated with Khat Use,* Research Report 44. London: United Kingdom Home Office.

UNITED STATES DEPARTMENT OF HOMELAND SECURITY
2010 *2009 Yearbook of Immigration Statistics*. Washington: Office of Immigration Statistics.

UNIVERSITY SAINS ISLAM MALAYSIA
2010 *Fatwa Management System* available at http://infad.usim.edu.my/modules.php?op=modload&name=News&file=article&sid=10334 (visited 30 November 2010)

VARISCO, Daniel M.
1986 'On the Meaning of Chewing of QAT (*Catha Edulis*) in the Yemen Arab Republic.' *International Journal of Middle East Studies* 18: 1-13.

WAGNER, Mark
2005 'The Debate between Coffee and Qat in Yemeni Literature.' *Middle Eastern Literatures* 8(2): 121-149.

WHO (WORLD HEALTH ORGANISATION)
2006 *WHO Expert Committee on Drug Dependence – 34th Report WHO Technical Report Series* 942-946.

LEGAL COMPLEXITY IN NATURAL RESOURCE MANAGEMENT IN THE FRONTIER MAHAKAM DELTA OF EAST KALIMANTAN, INDONESIA

Rikardo Simarmata

1. Introduction

As of the late 1960s, the Indonesian government has been practicing a policy of territorial zoning in the governing of natural resource use in the Mahakam Delta of East Kalimantan, Indonesia. The zoning of certain areas through various technical means, followed by the exercise of state jurisdiction over territorialized areas by creating regulations to delineate how and by whom the resource can be used, is a key instrument of what has been termed 'territorial strategy', a type of resource control strategy (Vandergeest and Peluso 1995: 387).[1] In the late 1960s, part of the Mahakam Delta area was declared a State Mining Zone (hereafter SMZ). Thirteen

[1] This article perceives the 'territorial strategy' as internal strategy. Internal strategy is distinguished from external strategy. External strategy deals with state boundaries, construction of national identity, or center-periphery relations (Vandergeest and Peluso 1995: 387). Internal territorial strategy refers to the modern state, to distinguish it from non-territorial strategy which was practiced by pre-colonial rulers. The rulers of the earlier period, instead of controlling resource use by practicing territorial strategy, controlled people by imposing obligatory taxes per head, or forced labor (Vandergeest and Peluso 1995: 390; Peluso and Vandergeest 2001: 774).

years later, in 1983, the entire delta area was also declared a State Forest Zone (hereafter SFZ). Following those two demarcations as state property, both the Ministry of Energy and Mineral Resources and the Ministry of Forestry have applied state laws and regulations to the use of resources in the Mahakam Delta. An important provision of those laws and regulations states that no use of natural resources in the area shall be undertaken without an official license, either from those two ministries or from the provincial and district government. A second key provision states that the use of resources shall protect the forest and the environment from destruction and degradation.

In practice however, the use of resources in the Mahakam Delta does not comply with these two provisions. Several resource tenure rights have been granted by central and local authorities. Yet the granting of rights is often not in accordance with existing laws and regulations; for example, the resource tenure rights given to pond owners in the SFZ were not awarded by the Forestry Minister, and thus do not follow forestry laws and regulations. The use of the Mahakam Delta's SFZ for oil and gas extraction is without a license of any kind. Most fishery resource use also occurs without a license. Such use of resources without strict accordance to existing laws and regulations, and without licenses from authoritative government agencies, indicates that the territorial strategy in the Mahakam Delta does not work. Further, such resource use has resulted in the destruction and degradation of the environment of the Mahakam Delta – in particular, the deforestation of its mangrove forest.[2] This deforestation has precipitated many additional ecological consequences for the delta, including a severe decline in fishing productivity (Noryadi et al. 2006), and increased sedimentation and seawater intrusion (Aspar in Kusumastanto and Bengen 2001: 28, Sidik 2009: 5).

This article argues that ineffective formal state control over coastal resource use and lack of application of formal rules does not necessarily lead to a situation where rules are absent. In reality, there exist widespread informal and semi-informal rules governing how coastal resources are allocated. There is customary law as practiced by local residents (*Buginese of Kalimantan*), and new informal rules brought to the area by recent immigrants (*Buginese of Sulawesi*). The semi-

[2] In 1996, the deforested area of the Mahakam Delta mangrove forest totalled 15,000 hectares. Three years later this had reached 67,000 hectares, and 85,000 hectares by 2001 (Duitrieux 2001: 64). In 2007 the Government of East Kalimantan Province estimated that deforestation totaled 90,000 hectares or 80% of the entire Mahakam Delta.

informal rules in the Mahakam Delta constitute the process by which local government officials establish their own interpretations of formal rules, which they use to authorize local tenure arrangements. In this respect, the semi-formal rules are a hybrid of informal (non-state) rules and re-interpreted formal (state) rules (Michaels 2009: 15). Thus all informal, semi-informal, and to a lesser extent formal rules co-exist, bringing about normative complexity of resource use arrangements in the Mahakam Delta.

This article examines the extent to which coastal use in the Mahakam Delta does not comply with formal rules. It aims to identify key factors that may have caused the formal rules to be ineffective, and investigates how and why the alternative semi-formal rules have evolved.

After the Introduction, the article will proceed with a brief account of the changes in natural resource use in the Mahakam Delta through the Kutai Sultanate period (late fifteenth to ninetieth century), colonial period (ninetieth century to 1942), and post Indonesia's independence in 1945. The article will then describe the present resource use rights in the Mahakam Delta, which are governed by formal, semi-formal and informal rules. The article will present the reasons given by local government officials for their decisions and actions related to authorizing actual resource use; and will examine these findings.

The Mahakam Delta

The Mahakam Delta is located at the mouth of Mahakam River, in the eastern part of Borneo Island. Administratively, the Delta is situated in the district of Kutai Kartanegara (henceforth Kutai district) in the province of East Kalimantan (henceforth 'the province'). Kutai district is known as the richest district in Indonesia in terms of annual budget. The delta is three hours by car and boat from the province's capital, Samarinda; and four hours from Tenggarong, the capital of Kutai district.

The delta comprises a chain of 92 islands (totalling 1,000km2), in addition to several tributary rivers and the coast (Bapedalda Kutai Kartanegara and PKSPL IPB 2002: III-64). The total delta, including islands, channels and coast, covers 1,500km2. The delta is situated across three sub-districts (Muara Badak, Anggana and Muara Jawa) which include eight villages and 12,000 people.

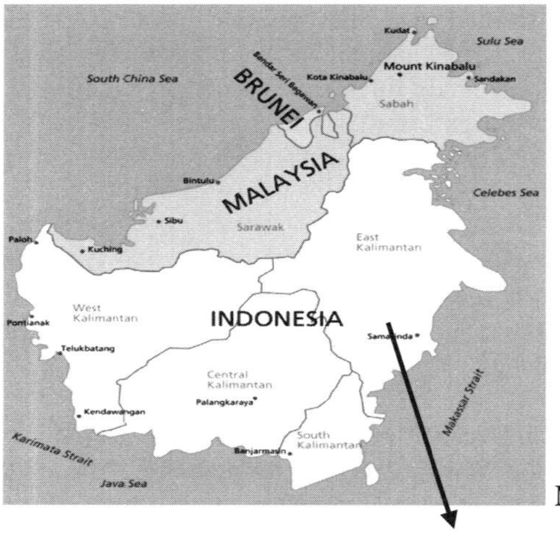

Map of Kalimantan Island

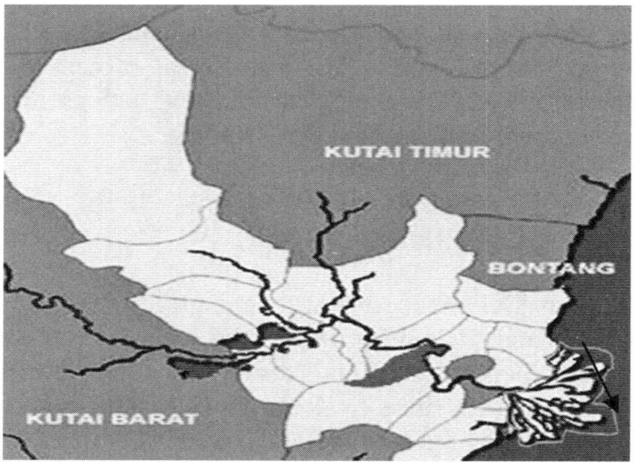

Mahakam Delta

2. Changing Resource Use

From the period of the Kutai Sultanate (late 15th century) to the present, the three main natural resources uses in the Mahakam Delta have been fishing, cultivation of fish (in ponds), and oil and gas extraction. Until the period of Dutch administration (1844-1942) two additional resource use sectors existed: rattan gathering and coconut planting (Levang 2002: 4). Rattan gathering declined during the timber boom in the late 1960s, driven also by increased central government control of rattan collection, purchase and sale in the early 1970s (Peluso 1983). With the extensive opening of fish ponds in 1997-2001, rattan gathering in the delta effectively ceased. Coconut planting also declined during the timber boom and the initiation of oil exploration in the early 1970s.

Concurrent with oil exploration and exploitation in the delta, the prospects for fishing improved due to increased international demand from Japan and elsewhere. In the 1970s, shrimp fishing in the Mahakam Delta and across Indonesia was conducted by trawling. Trawling was banned in the early 1980s because of its negative environmental and social impacts (Jhamtani 2003: 27; Bailey 1988: 13, 36). Some publications suggest a causal relationship between the trawl ban and the emergence of the shrimp ponds in the delta as the fishers required an alternative source of income.[3] However, shrimp ponds first emerged in the delta in the latter 1970s (Bourgeois et al. 2002: 36; Bapedalda Kutai Kartanegara and PKSPL IPB 2002: III-64), and pond development continued at low levels until the 1997 economic crisis, when a surge in shrimp export triggered an unsustainable boom in the number of ponds.

Cultivated fishing has declined since 2000, as productivity has decreased sharply. In the period 1996-1999, when pond productivity peaked, a one-hectare pond could yield 20-40kg of tiger shrimp and 600kg of wild shrimp and crabs (Bourgeois et al. 2002: 65) One study even predicted that a one-hectare pond could yield up to 200-1,000kg of tiger shrimp (Sumaryono et al. 2008: 25-26). More recently, productivity has fallen to only 21,5kg/ha and 24,5kg/ha for tiger shrimp and wild shrimp respectively (Noryadi et al. 2006).

3. Existing Use Rights

As the Mahakam Delta has been designated as state forest, all non-forestry activities, such as oil and gas extraction and other land uses, require licenses from the Minister of Forestry. However, this requirement is disregarded without penalty: Total E&P Indonesia, a French-Japanese joint venture oil and gas

[3] For example see Bapedalda Kutai Kartanegara and PKSPL IPB 2002: III-66, and Hidayati et al. 2005.

company[4], has been exploring and exploiting within the SFZ without a license. Land holders likewise occupy and cultivate the forests without licenses.[5] Similarly, most fishing in the delta is conducted without licenses from either the Ministry of Marine Affairs and Fisheries, the provincial governor or the district head (*bupati* or regent). Given that the formal licensing rules governing coastal resource use have not been effectively implemented, they have been replaced by other tenure arrangements involving informal and semi-informal rules. Except in the use of oil and gas resources, informal and semi-informal rules are the dominant determinants of coastal resource use and forest land distribution among users in the delta.

[4] The company was founded in 1968, a member of Total group, a French company operating in 130 countries. Due to its operations in the Mahakam Delta, Total E&P Indonesie is presently the biggest gas producer in Indonesia, producing 30% of Indonesia's gas production.

[5] According to Indonesian land law and administrative practices, tenure over land could have been acquired through either state law or *adat* customary law. A piece of land is titled land as long as it is supported by certain written documents, issued or signed by either the National Land Agency, head of district, head of sub-district or *adat* leader. The National Land Agency issues certificates; the head of district issues land reclamation permits; the head of the sub-district (together with the village head, head of hamlet (*ketua RT*) and *adat* leader) sign a land letter (Harsono 2005; Ilyas 2005). Titled land in the Mahakam Delta is supported primarily by land letters. Of the delta's 103,682ha of land, only 891 hectares were certified at the time of writing. In practice the difference between certified land and land supported by land letters is vague and confusing, particularly when undertaking land procurement. Many land procurement and other land transfer cases perceive the two to be similar, and assign them equal value with respect to compensation or sale prices (Sutedi 2007: 79, 129, 130). However, in other cases the two are perceived to be different, with *adat*-based titled land considered to be primarily state land, in which case a title holder is only entitled to compensation for trees and buildings above the land (Fitzpatrick 1997, 2007). For practical purposes, here I use the term 'land holder' to mean someone whose tenure over land is based on informal rule, either *adat* or another form of informal rule. This is distinguished from the term 'land owner,' which means someone whose tenure over land is based on formal land law.

3.1. Complex existing tenure arrangements

3.1.1. Oil and gas resources

During Dutch colonial rule, oil production was undertaken through a concession system. Pursuant to the *Indische Mijnwet* (Indies Mining Act) of 1899, concession holders owned all oil that they drilled, as they had paid land rent and royalty (Simamora 2000: 83). The amendment of the Mining Act in 1918 reduced the duration of the concession from 75 years to 40 (Lindblad 1989: 55). After oil was discovered in Tarakan and Balikpapan, two other prominent oil centers in East Kalimantan, mining companies, engineers and the Dutch government reduced their interest in offshore exploration in the Mahakam Delta area, which presented logistical and financial difficulties related to access, and the limited technology available for offshore exploration.

The exercise of state jurisdiction over petroleum resources in the Mahakam Delta commenced later than on the mainland, in the mid-1960s.[6] In 1967 the Indonesian central government and the Ministry of Mining awarded to Japan Petroleum Exploration (hereafter Japex) a large offshore area of the Mahakam Delta, including Tarakan Island. The area comprised 34,125 square kilometres, called the Mahakam-Bunyu block (Idham 1973: 125). The award comprised part of an exploration contract between Japex and the state-owned company Pertamina. Based on this contract, from 1966 onwards Japex undertook exploration of their work area, but failed to discover oil (Idham 1973: 125). In 1970, Japex (now renamed Inpex Corporation) handed over the work area to the French company Total E&P Indonesie[7], with an agreement between Inpex Corporation and Total E&P Indonesie in which the latter would be an operator and in which each company

---

[6] On the mainland petroleum, exploration commenced in the late 19th century (Magenda 1991: 10; Lindblad 1988: 32; Lindblad 1989: 53). In 1888 the Sultan of Kutai granted a large concession to a Dutch engineer, JH Menten, which was later split into three concessions, situated in the Sanga-Sanga district (Idham 1973: 119).

[7] Later this name was changed to Total E&P Indonesie. The company was founded in 1968 as a member of Total group, a worldwide French company operating in 130 countries. From its operation in the Mahakam Delta, Total E&P Indonesie is presently the biggest gas producer in Indonesia, yielding 30% of Indonesian gas production.

would have a 50% share.

As a contractor, Total E&P Indonesie (Total) has rights to explore and exploit oil and gas resources in the block, but it does not have ownership rights over the exploited oil and gas, as the rights still belong to the state. Total is, however, entitled to obtain cost recovery and profit sharing. To date, Total has been awarded four production sharing contracts (PSC) by the Indonesian government: Mahakam PSC (1970); Tengah JOB PSC (1988); Saliki PSC (1997); and Southeast Mahakam PSC (1998), covering an area of 5,962km2.

In 1983, nearly the entire area of the Mahakam Delta was officially declared an SFZ by the Ministry of Forestry. Following this ruling, Total E&P Indonesia and other companies are required to obtain a forest use permit from the Ministry of Forestry, before they can log trees inside the forest areas or use the areas for other activities. Any offence against this provision carries a sentence of up to ten years' jail or approximately US$950,000 in fines. At the time of this research, Total E&P Indonesia claimed to be writing a proposal for submission to the Ministry of Forestry. This proposal was still in draft form after 40 years of company operations in the delta, and 25 years after the enactment of the 1985 Government Regulations on forest protection forest, which legally obliged the company to possess a forest use permit before undertaking work.[8]

3.1.2. Land resources

According to the 1960 Act on Oil and Gas (now replaced by the Act of 2001), rights to explore and exploit oil and gas resources do not include rights over land (Kartasapoetra 1992: 15-16, 77, 80). If the land to be used by contractors is privately owned or state land that is being cultivated, the Act stipulates that contractors shall acquire the land through selling, exchange, compensation, recognition, or other exchanges, in negotiation with the land owners.

In the Mahakam Delta, the situation concerning land ownership is rather different; as nearly all the delta's area is SFZ. According to existing laws and regulations, certain land rights are precluded inside the SFZ, as all forest resource use shall be through license from the forestry minister, the provincial governor or the head of

[8] The Government Regulation of 1985 was more recently superseded by Government Regulation No. 45/2004.

Kutai district. In reality, the actions of Total and Upstream Oil and Gas Supervisory Agency (hereafter Executive Agency) suggest that land rights exist there. [9] Before paying compensation, Total and the Executive Agency required the land owners to present land certificates or a 'land letter'. Interestingly, they did not examine whether those lands were located inside or outside the SFZ. They also did not examine whether the land owners lived inside or outside the Mahakam Delta. An officer of Anggana sub-district explained the actions of Total and the Executive Agency as follows:

> They behave in this way not because they do not know that the land is located inside the Forest State Zone, but because they want to avoid a prolonged process. Instead of following legal rationale, they prefer to use economic rationale.

Only after land owners presented a land certificate or land letter would Total and the Executive Agency provide compensation. In arranging compensation, the two organizations considered land letters signed by village and sub-district government officers to be comparable with land certificates. Therefore, Total and the Executive Agency appear to consider that all people in the Mahakam Delta who can present these documents are land owners, rather than just land users. The documents are perceived to be proof that there are certain rights relationships between land holders and land. What are these documents actually? Why do they serve, as an instrument to denote the rights relationship?

3.1.2.1. Land letters

In 1972, the Minister of Home Affairs promulgated a decree authorizing a head of sub-district to issue a permit called a Land Reclamation License (*Izin Membuka Tanah).*[10] According to the decree, the maximum size of a piece of land that could

[9] Following the replacement of Oil and Gas Act of 1960 by Act of 2001 and the enactment of Government Regulation of 2002, all authority to control oil and gas contractors and to conduct PSC has been transferred from *Pertamina* to the Executive Agency.

[10] The Land Reclamation License originated from Land Reclamation Rights as stipulated in the 1960 Basic Agrarian Law. The Land Reclamation Rights originated from *adat* customary law, referred to as forest reclamation rights (Parlindungan 1986: 121; Harsono 2005). Forest reclamation rights are granted by

be given through the license was two hectares. The decree also stated that in issuing the license, a head of sub-district should heed advice from the village head. It could thus be argued that seeking such advice was a requirement to obtain the license. In practice however, this advice became standardized as a land letter (*surat keterangan tanah* or *surat tanah)*. The letter was also popularly known as a *leges* letter or *segel* letter. Land letters contain information about the owner, origin of the land, location, width, and actual usage of the land. Regarding the accuracy of information in the land letter, in some letters the village or sub-district head takes responsibility, and in others the owner takes responsibility. Every holder of a Land Reclamation License is entitled to benefit from and use the land.

In 1984, the Minister of Home Affairs issued an instruction to abolish the authority of heads of sub-districts to issue Land Reclamation Licenses. This means that as of 1984, a head of sub-district remains prohibited from issuing licenses. In 1995, a governor's decree stated that at the provincial level, the authority to sign or issue a letter confirming land rights now belongs to the village head.[11] Despite sub-district heads no longer having this authority, some sub-district heads, including those of Anggana and Muara Badak sub-districts, remain active in providing the land documents needed for compensation and donation. These documents comprise four separate papers: (1) a letter declaring a named person to be the owner of a certain piece of land (similar to a land letter): (2) a letter declaring that the land is undisputed; (3) a field observation report; and (4) a letter notifying that rights over the land have been transferred to a new owner. The first, second and fourth documents are required when land owners transfer (sell, inherit or expropriate) their land to others, and are signed by the sub-district head; the third is required to support the first, and may be signed by any official of the sub-district office.[12]

---

the *adat* community leader either to a member of the community, or to an outsider, to clear a piece of forest for agriculture. However the Basic Agrarian Law prioritized the administrative aspects of the provision of Land Reclamation Rights (Abdurrahman 1979: 16); and in the later regulations, Land Reclamation Rights were converted into a license instead of rights.

[11] The governor's decree is No. 31/1995 concerning guidance to carry out the reorganization of land letters.

[12] Before a sub-district head signs the first document, there should be a field check to verify the information provided by land holders. In practice, sub-district officers rarely attend field observations, as land holders do not have the finances to pay the officer for this duty. Instead sub-district heads rely on information provided by village government officers.

During land transfers to Total, it is thus evident that neither Total, the Executive Agency, nor village nor sub-district heads typically check whether land owners possess the required land rights or permits from the forestry minister, provincial governor or district head, despite the lands in question being situated within the SFZ. By paying compensation to land owners, Total and the Executive Agency appear to be acknowledging that land owners do have certain land use rights. Village and sub-district heads appear to acknowledge similar rights when they sign the aforementioned land documents and allow land owners to use and transfer land. In 2005, this acknowledgment at the local government level was actually strengthened by a verdict of Kutai district court,[13] which accepted local-level land documents as legal evidence proving rights of a certain piece of land. The case involved a land dispute between two big *punggawas* in the delta, who each claimed ownership of 500 hectares of land located in Muara Pantuan village, Anggana sub-district. Both the plaintiff and the defendant provided written evidence to support their claim. The defendant then provided a 1998 letter signed by the village and sub-district heads, which the judges accepted, awarding the land to the defendant. The verdict was upheld in 2007 by the East Kalimantan court of appeal.[14]

Regardless of government officials and Total's employees acknowledging land letters as legal documents, it is interesting to consider why sub-district heads continue to sign such land letters, despite their authority to do so having been withdrawn by the Ministry of Home Affairs in 1984. Questions also arise as to why Total's employees and government officials did not examine whether lands were located inside or outside the SFZ, nor ask land holders whether they had obtained particular rights or permits from the Ministry of Forestry to occupy the forest land. These questions suggest a deeper reason behind the official acknowledgment of the legality of land letters. One reason that government officials – particularly local government officials – have offered is that they consider land holders to have rights over their land based on their long residence in the delta, and because they cultivate and manage the lands in question.

Further investigation reveals how such land holders are able to claim rights over their forest land without compliance with forestry legislation. To some extent the land letter is simply an acknowledgement that a person is occupying and managing a particular plot of land. A letter does not deal with how someone should occupy, manage or possess the land. Therefore, in the Mahakam Delta these ownership

[13] Verdict No. 44/Pdt.G/2003/PN Tgr.

[14] Verdict No. 132/PDT/2006/PT.KT.SMDA.

issues, along with land transfers, have instead been managed according to local, informal and generally accepted rules.

One of these local rules is that anybody can occupy, manage and own a particular plot of land, unless somebody else has claimed it in advance. A plot of land which is not subject to a private claim is perceived to be state land, and is considered to be available for anyone to claim (Hidayati et al. 2005: 47). Plots of land that have been claimed (locally named *rintis*) are usually identified by particular physical marks, such as planted trees, or jacks tied around particular trunks. Village officials and their relatives are held to be the appropriate people with whom to speak, to obtain information about unclaimed land. In many cases, village heads authorize local farmers' associations to coordinate and distribute unclaimed land among their members. In a few cases, village heads have even granted rights to *punggawas* (patrons or heads of complex local networks) to control particular areas. Having such rights, the punggawas could distribute them to others or utilize them for their own use (Lenggono 2004: 114).

After exercising occupation and control over claimed plots of land, most land holders have not sought land letters, as they appear to believe that the physical marks used to identify the plot, in addition to the acceptance of neighbouring land holders, is sufficient to represent land ownership (Hidayati et al. n.d: 65). Yet some land holders will approach village heads to request a land letter. To obtain a land letter, land holders are required to present a sketch map of the claimed land, showing the size of the land and the names of holders of neighbouring lands. They also pay a small fee to obtain the land letter (approximately US$32 per letter).

In addition to these local rules, there are two other widely accepted rules by which to obtain land rights. Firstly, any land located directly behind the yard of a house is considered to belong automatically to the house's owner. Secondly, a person can buy claimed land. Recent migrants and outsiders have been the primary solicitors of such land from local villagers. Most of these financial transactions are supported only by receipts from the sellers; very few are supported by official documents or signatures from sub-district heads.

A desire to sell claimed land to outsiders is a common reason for land holders to attempt to acquire a land letter. Due to a spate of land disputes in which local villagers reoccupied land that they had previously sold to outsiders, many purchasers now demand a land letter from sellers, to strengthen their claims of rights over the purchased land. The other most common reason for arranging a land letter is to increase the likelihood of receiving compensation from companies interested in acquiring the land. As mentioned before, only if land holders can present land letters will Total and the Executive Agency compensate them. This requirement for a land letter (and identity card) refers to a decree by the head of the Executive Agency in 2007.[15] It was apparent during the research for this article that although most land holders felt secure with their customary evidence of land rights, they still accepted the need to fulfil the legal requirements for obtaining compensation for their land. They did not contest the requirement by arguing that their local informal rules awarded them sufficient rights over their land. Instead they continued to obtain land letters, despite the expense and length of the process.

It should be noted that the people of the Mahakam Delta do not merely consider land from an economic point of view; land is also embedded in their socio-cultural life. Some research has suggested that the construction of fish ponds is often an important prelude to marriage. When preparing a dowry for the family of a woman whom their son will marry, parents may construct numerous fish ponds in the hope of a high return from their harvest (Bapedalda Kutai Kartanegara and PKSPL IPB 2002: III-53). Another proposed reason for the escalation in pond construction is the desire to raise funds for a pilgrimage to Mecca. For the delta's Buginese people, although the hajj title (a title a Muslim will hold after conducting a pilgrimage to Mecca as a religious duty) has less religious meaning, it is still a social symbol which indicates financial success and demonstrates the holder's power over local tenure.[16]

3.1.3 Fishery Resources

In the Mahakam Delta, fisheries resources are almost always used without the provision of official rights by the provincial or Kutai district governments. Up to 2008, the Kutai District Fishery and Marine Affairs Agency had only ever granted two fishery licenses (*Surat Izin Usaha Perikanan*) neither of which was for an area located in the delta.[17] Agency data refer only indirectly to the fact that no local fisher in the delta possesses a fishery license for catching or cultivating fish. The delta fisheries are dominated not by local residents but by fishers from the upper

[15] See Number KEP-0113/BP00000/2007/S0 concerning guidance for land expropriation.

[16] See Wijaya n.d: 2.

[17] See Dinas Perikanan dan Kelautan Kutai Kartanegara 2008: 34-35.

Mahakam River and South Kalimantan, who have returned to using trawl nets following a lack of enforcement of the official ban (Hidayati et al. 2005: 52-62). According to one Kutai District Fishery and Marine Affairs Agency officer, the outside fishers do not possess the required permits either; merely a 'ship certificate', which does not include the right to exploit fishery resources.

The situation differs slightly between traditional fishers, and peasants who own ponds covering not more than two hectares. According to laws and regulations, these groups are not obliged to have a fishery license; instead they must have a kind of registration code (*Tanda Pencatatan Kegiatan Perikanan* or *TPKP*), issued by the Kutai district head. The TPKP must be renewed annually. During 1995-1997, 500 fishers and pond owners obtained the TPKP. After authority to issue TPKPs was transferred to sub-district heads in 2001, no renewal of TPKPs has been reported. To address this decreased compliance, the fishery agency created a registration program in collaboration with the District Public Transportation Agency, and in 2007 this joint program supported 300 fishers and pond owners in the delta in obtaining ship certificates from the public transportation agency. The fishery agency expected that after obtaining ship certificates, fishers and pond owners would register their fishery resource use; however, not a single person did so. A staff member from the sub-district fishery agency explained what they believed to be the reasons for the lack of registration:

> The fishermen were lazy and reluctant to register because they did not know the regulations, and more importantly because they knew they were not going to be punished for not having the registration code.

The official probably simplified when saying that a lack of knowledge of formal fishery rules, and a belief in a lack of enforcement, were the chief causes of non-compliance. A case involving static *julu* nets in Sepatin village demonstrates that legal non-complance is not always attributable to either of these reasons. Twice in 2009 a team of 20 personnel, including Total employees, regional and district officials, local military and police officers, visited Sepatin village to direct ten fishers to remove their *julu* nets from near Total's installation, under threat that officials would remove the *julu* gear themselves. The officials, military and police personnel stated a belief that the *julu* nets were installed against fishery and public navigation regulations. Yet eight of the ten fishers disobeyed the order. The reason they gave was that they deserved compensation for their *julu* nets. The fishers noted that local fishing rules concerning *julu* net has been long established, and appeared to call on the authority of these informal rules. An elder fisher of the group of ten *julu* owners said:

> Those julu fishing grounds have been inherited by our ancestors. Our ancestors have developed them since the first settlement was established in the Mahakam Delta. They have completely divided the water of the Pemangkaran through Sepatin into the julu fishing grounds.

According to local fishing rules, *julu* net owners are entitled to prohibit others from installing *julu* nets on their sites. In addition, an owner can sell or rent his fishing ground to others for a period of time. The local rules state that anyone can fish in any location, unless it disturbs another fisher who has already occupied a nearby fishing ground. The rules also specify a permitted fishing period, namely, 2 a.m. to 5 a.m. Given that these local fishing rules exist and are widely known, the elder fisher's statement challenges the perceptions of officials, who claimed to be suspicious that financial compensation was the real reason behind the continued instalment of the nets.

3.2. Prominent factors in the ineffectiveness of formal state control

From the above descriptions, it is clear that at the time of this research, formal state control over resource use in the Mahakam Delta's SFZ is ineffective, and legal regulations are being disregarded. Pond owners occupy and use the SFZ without rights or licenses from the forestry minister, provincial governor or Kutai district head, and their land use is supported instead by 'administrative documents' signed by village and sub-district government officers. Although Total, the Executive Agency, and provincial and Kutai district government officers do not consider these land documents as allotting full rights or licenses, in practice they have treated them as so. In addition to the absence of correct licenses for fisheries operations, Total itself has been operating in the Mahakam Delta's SFZ since the early 1970s without the required permit from the forestry minister.

This article develops a view that the aforementioned management failure is supported by two conditions: (1) the lack of legal implementation and law enforcement, and (2) administrative conflict about authority over forest management within the process of decentralization.

3.2.1. Lack of legal implementation and law enforcement

The lack of legal implementation and law enforcement in relation to land use in the Mahakam Delta's SFZ includes the following two management deficiencies: (1) lack of demarcation of land use zones; and (2) lack of surveillance and control of forest areas.

Regarding demarcation, in accordance with forestry laws and regulations, and in particular Government Regulation No. 33 of 1970 concerning forestry planning, the Ministry of Forestry should have delineated the declared production forest area in the delta, in order to clarify its legal status. However, demarcation activities for the production forest did not commence until 2000, seventeen years later. The main reason for the delay appears to be that priority was given to demarcating other SFZs on the mainland and the upper Mahakam River, where there are numerous timber concessions and small settlements which were perceived to be a threat to the timber concessions.

The provincial government began demarcating the production forest of the delta in 2001, following the 1999 decentralization, and encountered several obstacles. The provincial forestry service unit in charge of the demarcation, *Unit Pelaksana Teknis Daerah Planologi Samarinda* (hereafter *UPTD Planologi*) encountered serious budget constraints. The unit requested funding from the provincial government for demarcation activities several times, but each time both the provincial development planning agency and the provincial legislature rejected the proposals. *UPTD Planologi* was often also forced to compete for funding against another division of the provincial forestry agency, which also dealt with demarcation issues and tended to be awarded funding preferentially.

In an attempt to resolve its budget constraints, *UPTD Planologi* eventually submitted their budget proposal to the Ministry of Forestry. The proposal was approved, with the provision that demarcation was to be carried out in collaboration with *Balai Pemangkuan Kesatuan Hutan Region IV* (*BPKH*), a service unit of the Ministry of Forestry based in the province. Despite these obstacles, by 2005 the *UPTD Planologi* had completed most of the demarcation of the delta's SFZ. Budget shortages prevented full demarcation, but 81,180.80 hectares (94% of the delta's total forest land) was demarcated, with several smaller islands being excluded (Tim Sosialisasi 2008: 20).

With respect to formal law enforcement and land use in the SFZ, the second management deficiency relates to surveillance and control, neither of which was effectively implemented in the delta. Between 1965 and 1998, responsibility for protection of the delta's SFZ belonged to *KPH/CDK Mahakam Ilir*, another service unit of the provincial forestry agency. *CDK Mahakam Ilir* has responsibility for 676,528 hectares across East Kalimantan, 3% of the total land area. Of this area, about 9 per cent (75,200 hectares) is mangrove forest, most of which is reported to be in the Mahakam Delta. During the 1980s and 1990s, 17 timber concessions and 31 sawmills and plywood companies existed within *CDK Mahakam Ilir*'s managed area.

None of the annual reports of *CDK Mahakam Ilir* mentions surveillance activities in the Mahakam Delta's SFZ. For example in the 1999-2000 report, at a time when pond development was flourishing in the delta, there is not a single word about the delta. Very few annual reports provide information about forest resource use or management. The 2002 report briefly mentions surveillance activity to manage forest fires and forest occupation, but does not refer to the delta as a place where surveillance occurred.[18]

A former head of Muara Badak and Samboja forestry offices acknowledged that during his terms (1985-1989 and 1999-2002) he never visited the Mahakam Delta, despite it falling under his authority. The head of forestry offered several reasons why he did not direct his men to enforce the laws on pond ownership, including: insufficient officers (six men); high shrimp prices; a situation in which several villages were found before he was assigned to his position,[19] and uncertainty regarding whether pond owners had official permits. Another forestry staff member mentioned that he had never visited any of the delta's islands for surveillance purposes, but that during a sailing holiday he had visited two islands, noticed the many new ponds, and reported these to his supervisor. The supervisor submitted the report to more senior management, but there was no response nor action taken.

In addition to the abovementioned factors, another prominent institutional factor

---

[18] See Dinas Kehutanan UPTD Peredaran Hasil Hutan Samarinda 2003: 2.

[19] A similar reason was offered by forestry officials whose jurisdiction included a collaborative management initiative in Gunung Halimun-Salak National Park, West Java. The officials claimed they did not enforce the laws with local villagers who cultivated rice paddies and vegetables and harvested forest products, because the villagers had practiced this livelihood before the park was established (Kubo 2010: 244).

which hampers effective surveillance and control is the pro-timber orientation of the government management agencies. The organizational structure of the service units *CDK Mahakam Ilir* (later re-named *UPTD PHH Samarinda*) and *UPTD Planologi* indicate that both units were designed to serve and support the timber concessions. For example, the sub-district offices of both service units were always established in areas with timber concessions, and their checking offices only occurred on log-truck routes. The organizational structures of both units clearly imply that they focus primarily on protecting forest concessions and ensuring that trees are transported and sold legally.

Such pro-timber oriented management in the delta may explain why production forest over which government has not granted rights or permits has been overlooked by local officials.[20] Some local officials have claimed, incorrectly, that the delta's mangrove forest is conversion production forest.[21] It is more surprising that in the *UPTD Mahakam Ilir*'s annual reports, the delta's SFZ is not marked as part of their area.

3.2.2. Administrative conflict about authority over forest management

The forest management failures in the Mahakam Delta are attributable not only to the lack of implementation and enforcement of law, but also to administrative conflict over forest management. Major conflict arose in 2000 when the provincial

---

[20] In the early 1070s, the central government granted mangrove forest areas in northern East Kalimantan to four timber companies: Karyasa Kencana, Bina Lestari, Inhutani, and Jamaker. The total area of those four forest concessions is 213,040 hectares (Soetrisno 2007: 12). Prior to that time, the Dutch colonial government and the Sultan of Kutai had granted a forest concession to a Philippines company in the first half of the 20th century (Lindblad 1988; Obidzinski 2003).

[21] This misperception was also held by the provincial forestry officials, including the former head of the provincial forestry agency, who commented to local press that the mangrove forest's status was conservation forest but then 'corrected' himself to say that it was production forest. See *Kaltim Post*, Delta Mahakam, Kewenangan Pusat, 23 September 2003, and *Kaltim Post*, Mahakam Jadi Hutan Produksi, 19 May 2004. A higher official of the Ministry of Forestry also misunderstood the status of the delta's mangrove forest, thinking it to be a protected area.

government refused to hand over nine forests areas to the Kutai district government. Since 2000, the Kutai district government had been calling for the provincial government to transfer to them the authority over the forest areas, including the production forest of the delta. The Kutai district government cited two reasons for the transfer of the authority: (1) a 1995 commitment by the provincial government to hand over the nine forest areas at some late time; and (2) their interpretation of national and regional legislation regarding the transfer of government affairs, which states that authority over forest areas should be transferred from provincial to district government once the latter has established a forestry agency and the former has dismissed their district-based service units.[22]

In response to the Kutai district government's request, the provincial government declined to transfer authority for forest management, citing legislation to back their own position, including the provincial regulations of 1981, 1987 and 2001[23]. The provincial government's forestry agency argued that, regardless of the fact that the district government had established their own forestry agency in 1995, authority for forest areas could be retained by the provincial government because their district-based service units had not been dismissed and were still in force.

Frustration with the process led the Kutai district government to establish a branch in Muara Badak sub-district in 2003, in the hope that this would force the provincial government to transfer authority. To date this strategy has failed, and the provincial forestry unit remains the authority in the area. Since 2003, officers of the Kutai district government have stated publicly that they cannot do more to protect the Mahakam Delta's SFZ, beyond advising pond owners and undertaking rehabilitation to limit forest damage, until the provincial government officially transfers its authority over the areas.

Following these statements from Kutai district officers, some provincial government officers expressed surprise and stated that they believed the Kutai

[22] The national legislative provisions are Government Regulation No. 8/1995 and directive of the Ministry of Internal Affair No. 5/1995, whereas the regional provisions are Provincial Regulation No. 02/1995 and decree of provincial head of forestry agency No. 5223/579/DK-IV/1998.

[23] Those three provincial regulations are respectively No. 13/1981, 4/1987 and 2/2001, concerning the structure of provincial government organization.

district government already shared the authority and responsibility for the forest areas. They pointed to Government Regulation No. 62/1998, by which the Ministry of Forestry handed a total of nine forestry responsibilities over to the district government, including responsibility for forest protection.

This ongoing administrative disagreement has led to mutual suspicion between provincial-level and Kutai district government officers. Kutai officers suspect that the provincial government refuses to transfer authority for the forest areas because by doing so, they would lose control over several timber industries as well as their authority to issue recommendations for mining and oil concessions. However, officers from the provincial government and the Ministry of Forestry suggest that district government officers may have two hidden agendas. Firstly, they suggest that district officers may want broader control over the delta area; and they support their view by asserting that Kutai district officers are deliberately allowing people to use and deforest the SFZ as a prelude to requesting the Forestry Minister to release the areas from the SFZ.[24] Secondly, they note that several high-ranking Kutai district officers actually have ponds in the delta.

4. Administrative Culture of Justification

The final section of this paper examines the administrative culture of justification regarding government agencies' failures to manage the use of resources in the Mahakam Delta formally or effectively.

It is clear that at least some officials at central government level in Indonesia were aware of the failures in the delta, and expressed their concerns directly to local officials. In one case in July 2007, an official from the central Ministry of Forestry attended a coordination meeting jointly sponsored by Total, Inpex Corporation, and the Kutai district government, and strongly warned the provincial and Kutai government officials present, advising them to reconsider their proposal to convert parts of the delta's mangrove forest into non-forest area. The central government official argued that such forest conversion would raise environmental concerns and might expose Indonesia to negative international pressure. On another occasion, an official from the National Land Agency warned local officials from the Kutai district fishery agency that all fish ponds in the Mahakam Delta were illegal, and

[24] Some Ministry of Forestry officials made similar allegations against the Kutai district officials.

that if agency officials assisted the shrimp farmers they would be assisting in illegal activities.

Given that at least some officials from central government ministries drew on formal, legal rules and international expectations when advising how to deal with resource management in the delta, it is interesting to consider how closely the views of local government officials, particularly street-level bureaucrats, matched those of higher-level government. The findings of this research suggest that officials who interact directly with shrimp farmers and fishers, and observe the abundant and widespread ponds in the delta, have developed very different views from central government officials, which have shaped their management decisions and actions. [25]

This section examines four aspects of behaviour and decision-making that local officials tend to employ when managing the delta's natural resources. These are: (1) the use by officials of economic and social reasoning rather than legal argument to justify official decisions; (2) their interpretation of existing laws and regulations; (3) the permissive behaviour of street-level bureaucrats; and (4) their recognition of local rules concerning land and fish resources use. These four aspects are described below.

4.1. Economic and Social Considerations

There appear to be three reasons why village heads in the Mahakam Delta continue to sign land documents for development activities, particularly fish ponds, in the delta. Firstly they are simply continuing a tradition. The second reason relates to historical and sociological factors; namely that land holders have resided in the delta for a long time, and are perceived by the officials to be controlling and cultivating the land. The third and most important reason is economic: the ponds generate an income for local people. Village and district agency officers have observed that for some local people their ponds are their entire livelihood, and for others the ponds have at least improved their economic position. The Head of

[25] The term 'street-level bureaucrats' refers to the officers of the Kutai district agencies, village and sub-district governments. This is similar to Lipsky's (1980: 3) use of the term 'street-level bureaucrats' to refer to public service workers who interact directly with citizens in the course of their jobs, and who have substantial discretion in the execution of their work.

Muara Pantuan village stated:

> I like outsider investors (people who want to buy land in the Mahakam Delta for ponds) coming to our village, as they will bring money so that the villagers' economic position will improve.

Moreover, according to the officers, the removal of land holders and pond owners would require a large financial outlay, as the government would need to pay compensation.

An officer of the Kutai District Fishery and Marine Affairs Agency revealed the reasons why his agency did not prohibit fishermen in the delta from using trawls. He stated that it was because the fishermen are poor people, and the numbers of fishers are already big; and because, in his opinion, "handling trawl users is not the same as handling a thief". In addition to these reasons for inaction, there is also a perceived requirement that the government must provide an alternative source of income.

4.2. Interpretation of Existing Laws and Regulations

The head of Anggana sub-district has claimed that his signing of land documents did not constitute a violation of existing laws and regulations. He has pointed out two reasons to justify his view. Firstly he claims that, in his perception, signing the documents does not mean that land owners have ownership rights. Instead, land owners only have rights to cultivate the land. Therefore, as the existing laws and regulations only forbid him from granting ownership rights, he believes that he did not break the law. Secondly, he claims that by signing the documents he does not "issue" or authorize any license or rights, because his role in signing the documents is only the role of a witness. He states that he has always considered that the first and the second land documents are no more than statements from land owners that they do indeed cultivate their land. However, such an interpretation has been disputed by an officer of Muara Badak sub-district, who acknowledges that the signing of land documents by a sub-district head means that he or she does issue and authorize a permit, or at least provides a strong recommendation. Interestingly, this official still stated the belief that signing land documents was not a violation of existing laws and regulations, and gave two reasons. First, there had been no objection from superior officers from either the Kutai district government or the National Land Agency, nor had they reminded officials not to sign the documents.[26] Second, the practice continued because officials felt they had a consensus with local villagers. Beside those two reasons, the official stated:

> If we ask the land owners to comply with all legal requirements, that process will take a long time, and moreover the land owners will possibly protest while asking why the government officers did not previously inform them ahead about the requirements. Besides, we also feel that imposing the existing laws and regulations strictly would be sometimes culturally improper when the applicants are older men or community leaders.

Legal interpretations are also used to explain the absence of surveillance and enforcement in the Mahakam Delta's SFZ. A former head of the provincial forestry unit claims to have reached an interesting interpretation of the law. According to him, the ponds in the Mahakam Delta are not illegal for each of three reasons. First, he perceives the documents as being equivalent to a timber or mining extraction permit, and therefore the legal status of the land resource use as similar to the legal status of a forest and a mining concession. Second, when constructing ponds, the local people only cut nypah palm, which is not included in the Ministry of Forestry's list of 'forest products', and therefore the land owners are not violating any formal rules. Third, the nypah palms cut by the local people are not sold, and thus the people are not engaged in any illegal forest trade.

In August 2008, a team established by the head of the Kutai district, comprised predominantly of officers from the various Kutai agencies involved in the issue, conducted a 'socialization activity' in Anggana and Muara Jawa sub-districts. The main task of this team was to 'socialize' or highlight the importance of the delta's mangrove ecosystem to the local people, and to inform them of its legal status. At that meeting, the deputy head of the Kutai district agency explained to land owners and pond workers that they had illegally entered and occupied the Mahakam Delta's SFZ, because they did not possess a license from the governor, the head of

[26] This claim is contested by a statement from a high-ranking officer of the Kutai district government, who stated that they had warned the sub-district head several times not to sign any land letters for land located within a forest zone. He added that sub-district heads claimed they had difficulty following this directive, because land holders would ask them to point out the physical signs of the borders of the state forest, which they were unable to do.

the Kutai district or the forestry minister. Therefore according to existing laws and regulations, certain sanctions could be imposed upon them. However, the deputy head then stated that as the numbers of ponds had become enormous, the government would not ask people to leave the delta's SFZ. He said that in exchange for this leniency, and given that pond owners had deforested the area, they were responsible for rehabilitating the forest.

4.3. The Permissive Behaviour of Street-Level Bureaucrats

Street-level bureaucrats are also known as field officers. In the Mahakam Delta, their behaviour and decisions have greatly strengthened the perceived legitimacy of resource use rights, especially land use rights. The delta's field officers or street-level bureaucrats tend to avoid discussion about the legal status of the delta's ponds when they are conducting routine jobs such as assisting local people to plant mangrove tress. When pond owners or pond guards have asked about the land's legal status, the officers have been reported as saying only that it is not within their authority to answer such questions, because their job only deals with technical matters. The reasons for this avoidance may include the reasons proposed above by the district agency officers that ponds were established before the officers had been assigned to their current positions; and claims of official uncertainty over whether land holders may indeed have had license to cultivate (in Indonesian *izin* or *hak garap*).

When officers of the Ministry of Forestry service unit *UPTD Planologi* were undertaking the long-awaited demarcation of the protected zone, they deliberately avoided potential confrontations with land owners and pond workers. During the officers' work, whenever land owners or pond workers asked the purpose of the officers' visit, they avoided explaining the actual purpose of their activity, and instead claimed they were simply measuring and mapping the area. The officers even persuaded owners and workers that their activity would not affect the existence of ponds, by saying that they would not measure the inside sections of ponds, but only the outside sections.

A field officer from the district forestry agency in Muara Badak sub-district, who is also a member of the forestry police (*polisi kehutanan*), reported that he saw many instances of people cutting mangrove trees in the vicinity of Total installations. Although he confirms that he knew this was illegal, he did not take any action. His excuse for this inaction was that he was borrowing a boat from a local fisher and believed that if he detained the loggers and confiscated their chainsaw, they could potentially harm the boat owner in retribution, as they would recognize to whom the boat belonged.

In addition to economic and administrative factors, and potentially factors associated with self-interest, local officials frequently argued that their management decisions and actions were acceptable according to "rule norms", including both formal and informal rules. However, with respect to the formal rules, local officials have deliberately or inadvertently created new interpretations of the laws, in favour of the shrimp farmers' interests, and in opposition to the interpretations intended by central government officials. These new interpretations are clearly against the objectives of forest protection, which include preventing forest depletion by human activities, and security of state property such as the forests. Unclear or ambiguous wording of existing laws may have contributed to inadvertent misinterpretation of the formal rules.

In contrast to the lack of attention which local officials paid to the formal rules, it is clear that the officials were not only aware of, but strongly influenced by, local informal rules regarding land and fishery management. When village and sub-district heads signed land letters to confirm land rights, in each case they were abiding by the local informal rules concerning property rights, as earlier described. This research found no instances in which land letters were signed for land that was not already considered to belong to the letters' applicants, according to local rules. It is also apparent that these informal property rules do more than regulate the relationships between people and their land; they also regulate social norms between and among persons with respect to possessions (Benda-Beckmann and Benda-Beckmann 1994: 20-23; Hanna et al. 1996). Evidence of this is the statement by one official from Muara Badak sub-district, who said he could not refuse to sign a land letter presented to him, as it would be considered culturally improper. Thus, it is not only the informal rules regarding land ownership and use which pose a challenge to formal land management in the delta; informal rules regarding social correctness may pose an additional challenge.

5. Concluding Remarks

This article has identified and examined the many factors and conditions which impede the implementation and enforcement of formal resource tenure rights in the Mahakam Delta. As a result of these factors, the policy of territorial zoning does not meet its goals. Most resource use occurs without an official permit or license, and the ecology of the Mahakam Delta has been significantly degraded.

Many studies have attempted to explain the factors hampering the effectiveness of formal natural resource regulations in East Kalimantan. As Manning (1971: 14, 59) and Obidzinski (2003: 120) have observed, the Ministry of Forestry has hardly ever been able to implement government regulations over the SFZ in East Kalimantan. This is due partly to a lack of manpower, and partly to the fact that the power to do so rested with military and bureaucratic leaders in Jakarta, who have had other priorities. Vargas (1985) provided a clear case study of how a big forest company was required to deal directly with a Dayak indigenous community and migrant groups which lived within and near the company's forest interests, because of a lack of adequate involvement by Ministry of Forestry and other local officers.[27] The company contended directly with 'pirate' activities by the immigrant groups (Vargas 1985: 175, 249), and also dealt directly with the indigenous community regarding compensation for tress and crops; only afterwards reporting the results to sub-district government officers (Vargas 1985: 170).[28]

Despite some suggestions that resource use in the Mahakam Delta occurs without property arrangements (so-called open access), this study indicates that despite a lack of application of formal rules, resource use in the delta is regulated by complex rule arrangements.[29] Informal, semi-formal and formal rules co-exist. Local residents and new immigrants are capable to create rules concerning land rights, and the migrant Buginese people may have brought their own rules, to be applied fully or partly in the delta (Benda-Beckmann et al. 2005: 18). Other researchers have also reported that once a local shrimp farming community interacts with a larger social arena which favours formal rules and authority, the shrimp farmers may voluntarily accept the application of formal authority over their land rights (Moore 1978: 56).

---

[27] The company is PT International Timber Corporation Indonesia (ITCI). This company was a joint venture company of Weyerhaeuser Company of the United States, and PT Tri Usaha Bhakti of Indonesia. In 1971 the company was awarded a 601,100 hectare, 20-year timber concession in East Kalimantan. Most of this land was located in the Kutai district.

[28] For further information about how heavily Indonesian forestry officials relied on the timber concessionaries, see World Bank 1990: xxii.

[29] For the full account of the open access on land resource use in the Mahakam Delta, see Bourgeois et al. 2002: 2, 24; and Hidayati et al. 2004: 98.

The *jul* net case described in this study likewise exemplifies the application of formal rules to manage the use of fish resources, and their use by officials to supersede local fishing rules. In contrast, with respect to managing land arrangements, officials appear to use semi-formal rather than formal rules to provide authorization over informal land rights. A major challenge for officials is that nearly all the delta's shrimp ponds are located illegally inside the production forest. In response to this, local officials have created new interpretations of existing formal rules, in an apparent attempt to make their authorization efforts legitimate. Thus their authorization of resource use is often based on a misrepresentation of the formal rules. In particular, their authorization of land letters is largely against forestry legislation. In Indonesia, such local administrative discretion may have emerged to provide land tenure security over the million hectares of land which are not yet titled in accordance with Basic Agrarian Law, and which have already lost their established *adat* arrangements. In many areas of Indonesia, these semi-formal land and resource rights are obtained and managed through local-level negotiation (Fitzpatrick 2007: 139, 141).

This study illustrates the fluid nature of land tenure arrangements and use in the Mahakam Delta, as exemplified by land holders' voluntary acceptance of the application of the re-interpreted formal rules by local officials, and at the same time their acceptance of local officials' authorization. Land arrangements are negotiable and flexible (Peters 2006: 87-88), and dominated by informal and semi-formal rules at the expense of existing laws (Griffiths 1986; Benda-Beckmann and Benda-Beckmann 2006: 19). Although the co-existence of plural land arrangements appears acceptable to both land holders and local officials, with respect to fishery arrangements the co-existence of different sets of rules is more strongly contested. The disputes over the validity of formal and informal rules are not only between resource users and local officials; they also occur between levels of government, with central government officials citing formal laws as evidence that local officials' authorization of local land arrangements is illegal. Thus, the government itself is internally plural with respect to rules, a factor which greatly increases the challenges to Indonesia's effective and sustainable management of its natural resources.

References

ABDURRAHMAN, S.

1979 *Ketentuan-Ketentuan Pokok tentang Masalah Agraria, Kehutanan, Pertambangan, Transmigrasi dan Pengairan*. Bandung: Alumni.

BAILEY, Conner

1988 'The Political Economy of Marine Fisheries Development in Indonesia.' *Indonesia* 46: 25-38.

BAPEDALDA KUTAI KARTANEGARA and PKSPL IPB

2002 *Dampak Kegiatan Tambak Terhadap Kegiatan Minyak dan Gas di Delta Mahakam*. Unpublished report.

BENDA-BECKMANN, Franz von and Keebet von BENDA-BECKMANN

1994 *Property Rights and Economic Development*. London: Kegan Paul International.

2006 'The Dynamics of Change and Continuity in Plural Legal Orders.' *Journal of Legal Pluralism*, 53-54: 1-44.

BENDA-BECKMANN, Franz von, Keebet von BENDA-BECKMANN and Anne GRIFFITHS

2005 'Mobile People, Mobile Law: An Introduction.' Pp. 1-25 in Franz von Benda-Beckmann, Keebet von Benda-Beckmann and Anne Griffiths (eds.), *Mobile People, Mobile Law Expanding Legal Relations in a Contracting World*. Aldershot and Burlington VT: Ashgate.

BOURGEOIS, Robin, Fazrin RAHMADANI, Edi SUDIONO and Budi SULISTIADI

2002 *A Socio-Economic and Institutional Analysis of Mahakam Delta Stakeholders*. Unpublished report.

DINAS KEHUTANAN UPTD PEREDARAN HASIL HUTAN SAMARINDA

2003 *Laporan Tahunan (Dalam Angka)*. Unpublished report.

DINAS PERIKANAN DAN KELAUTAN KUTAI KARTANEGARA

2008 *Laporan Tahunan Dinas Perikanan dan Kelautan 2007*. Unpublished report.

DUITRIEUX, E

2001 'The Mahakam Delta Environment, from the '80's up to now: A Synthesis of a 15-year investigation.' Presented at an international workshop, *Optimizing Development and Environmental Issues of Coastal Area: Problem and Solution for Sustainability of Mahakam Delta*. Ministry of Marine Affairs and Fisheries, The Republic of Indonesia, and Center for Coastal and Marine Resources Studies, Bogor Agricultural University.

FITZPATRICK, Daniel

1997 'Dispute and Pluralism in Modern Indonesian Law.' *Yale Journal of International Law* 23: 171-212.

2007 'Land, custom, and the state in post-Suharto Indonesia: a comparative legal perspective.' Pp. 116-135 in Jamie S. Davidson and David Henley (eds.) *The Revival of Tradition in Indonesian Politics the Deployment of Adat from Colonialism to Indigenism*. Abingdon and New York: Routledge.

GRIFFITHS, John

1986 'What is Legal Pluralism?' *Journal of Legal Pluralism* 24: 1-55.

HANNA, Susan S., Carl FOLKE and Karl-Goran MALER (eds.)

1996 *The Rights to Nature: Cultural, Economic, Political and Ecological Principles of Institutions for the Environment*. Washington DC: Island Press.

HARSONO, Boedi

2005 *Hukum Agraria Indonesia Sejarah Pembentukan Undang-Undang Pokok Agraria, Isi dan Pelaksanaannya*. Jakarta: Djambatan.

HIDAYATI, Denny, Herry YOGASWARA, Fitranita, L. NAGIB, S.S. PURWANINGSIH and WIDAYATUN

2004 *Aspek Sosial Sensus Biota Laut Delta Mahakam dan Berau*. Jakarta: Lembaga Ilmu Pengetahuan Indonesia.

HIDAYATI, Denny, Herry YOGASWARA and Eniarti DJOHAN

2005 *Manajemen Konflik Stakeholders Delta Mahakam*. Jakarta: Lembaga Ilmu Pengetahuan Indonesia.

HIDAYATI, Denny et al.

n.d. *Status Tanah, Legalitas Penguasaan dan Pemilikan Lahan di Delta Mahakam*. Lembaga Ilmu Pengetahuan Indonesia (forthcoming).

IDHAM, Mohammad

1973 'Monografi Daerah Kabupaten Kutai tahun 1973'.

ILYAS

2005 *Konsepsi Hak Garap atas Tanah Dalam Sistem Hukum Pertanahan Indonesia dalam Kaitannya dengan Ajaran Negara Kesejahteraan*. PhD thesis at the University of Padjajaran, Bandung, Indonesia.

JHAMTANI, Hira (ed.)

2003 *Revolusi Biru Menebar Udang. Menuai Bencana*. Jakarta: Kophalindo.

KARTASAPOETRA, G, R.G. Kartasaputra, and A.G. Kartasaputra

1986 *Masalah Pertanahan di Indonesia*. Jakarta: Bina Aksara.

KUBO, Hideyuki

2010 'Understanding Discretionary Decision Making of Frontline Bureaucrats in State Forestland Management: A Case from Java, Indonesia.' *Society and Natural Resources* 23: 240-253.

LENGGONO, S. Pulenggono

2004 *Modal Sosial dalam Pengelolaan Tambak Studi Kasus pada Komunitas Petambak di Desa Muara Pantuan, Kecamatan Anggana, Kabupaten Kutai Kertanegara*. Master's thesis at Institut Pertanian Bogor.

LEVANG, Patrice

2002 *Mangroves, Shrimps and Punggawa A Historical Analysis of the Development of the Mahakam Delta*. Unpublished paper.

LINDBLAD, J. Thomas

1988 *Between Dayak and Dutch. The Economic History of Southeast Kalimantan 1880-1942*. Dordrecht: Foris Publications.

1989 'The Petroleum Industries in Indonesia before the Second World War.' *Bulletin of Indonesian Economic Studies* 25:52-76.

LIPSKY, Michael

1980 *Street-Level Bureaucracy: Dilemmas of the Individual in Public Serv*ices. New York: Russell Sage Foundation.

KUSUMASTANTO, Tridoyo and Dietrich G. BENGEN (eds.)

2001 *Optimizing Development and Environmental Issues of Coastal Area: Problem and Solution for Sustainable of Mahakam Delta*, Proceedings of an international workshop, Ministry of Marine Affairs and Fisheries The Republic of Indonesia and Center for Coastal and Marine Resources Studies, Bogor Agricultural University, Jakarta 4-5 April.

MAGENDA, Burhan

1991 *East Kalimantan The Decline of a Commercial Aristocracy*. Ithaca New York: Southeast Asia Study Program Cornell University.

MANNING, Chris

1971 'The Timber Boom with Special Reference to East Kalimantan.' *Bulletin of Indonesian Economic Studies* 7: 30-59.

MICHAELS, Ralf

2009 'Global Legal Pluralism.' *Duke Law School Faculty Scholarship Series*. Paper 185.

MOORE, Sally Falk

1978 *Law as Process: An Anthropological Approach*. London: Routledge and Kegan Paul.

NORYADI, Bambang I. GUNAWAN, Asfie MAIDIE, Iwan SUYATNA, A. Syafei SIDIK and SURIPNO

2006 *Studi Produktivitas Tambak di Kawasan Delta Mahakam Kalimantan Timur*. a final report submitted to Tota E&P Indonesie.

OBIDZINSKI, Krystof

2003 *Logging in East Kalimantan, Indonesia The Historical Expedience of*

Illegality. PhD thesis at the University of Amsterdam, the Netherlands.

PARLINDUNGAN, A.P.
1986 *Komentar atas Undang-Undang Pokok Agraria*. Bandung: Alumni Bandung.

PELUSO, Nancy Lee
1983 'Networking in the Commons: A Tragedy for Rattan.' *Indonesia* 35: 95-108.

PELUSO, Nancy Lee and Peter VANDERGEEST
2001 'Genealogies of the Political Forest and Customary Rights in Indonesia, Malaysia, and Thailand', *The Journal of Asian Studies* 60: 761-812.

PETERS, Pauline E.
2006 'Beyond Embeddedness: A Challenge Raised by a Comparison of the Struggles over Land in African and Post-Socialist Countries.' Pp. 84-105 in Franz and Keebet von Benda-Beckmann and Melanie G. Wiber, *Changing Properties of Property*. New York, Oxford: Berghahn Books.

SIDIK, Syafei Ahmad
2008 'The Changes of Mangrove Forest Ecosystem in Mahakam Delta, Indonesia: A Complex Social-Environmental Pattern Linkages in Resources Utilization.' Presented at The South China Sea Conference 'The South China Sea: Sustaining Ocean Productivities, Maritime Communities and the Climate', Kuantan, Malaysia, 25-29 November 2008.

SIMAMORA, M. Rudi
2000 *Hukum Minyak dan Gas Bumi*. Jakarta: Penerbit Djambatan.

SOETRISNO, Kadar
2007 'Hutan Mangrove Kalimantan Timur: Fungsi, Manfaat dan Kondisinya Saat Ini', inaugural speech of professorship, 19 April.

SUMARYONO
2008 *Pencitraan Kawasan Tambak di Delta Mahakam.* Dinas Perikanan dan Kelautan Kabupaten Kutai Kartanegara Provinsi Kalimantan Timur.

SUTEDI, Adrian
2007 *Peralihan Hak atas Tanah dan Pendaftarannya*. Jakarta: Sinar Grafika.

TIM SOSIALISASI KAWASAN DELTA MAHAKAM
2008 *Laporan Sosialisasi Kawasan Delta Mahakam*. Unpublished report..

VANDERGEEST, Peter and Nancy Lee PELUSO
1995 'Territorialization and State Power in Thailand', *Theory and Society* 24: 385-426.

VARGAS, Donna Mayo
1985 *'The Interface of Customary and National Land in East Kalimantan, Indonesia'*. PhD thesis at Yale University.

WIJAYA, Akhmad
2009 'Sosiologi Haji dalam Kultur Masyarakat Bugis di Delta Mahakam.' Unpublished paper.
WORLD BANK
1990 *Indonesia. Sustainable Development of Forests, Land, and Water*. A World Bank Country Study. Washington DC: The World Bank.

The Journal of Legal Pluralism and Unofficial Law
published by the Foundation for the Journal of Legal Pluralism
Editor in Chief: Gordon R. Woodman (Professor of Comparative Law, University of Birmingham)

Gordon R. Woodman (Editor in Chief)
The Journal of Legal Pluralism and Unofficial Law 59/2009
Bd. 59, 2010, 192 S., 29,90 €, br., ISBN 3-643-99917-7

LIT Verlag Berlin – Münster – Wien – Zürich – London
Auslieferung Deutschland / Österreich: siehe Impressumsseite